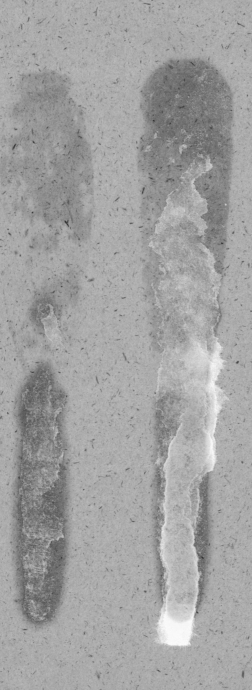

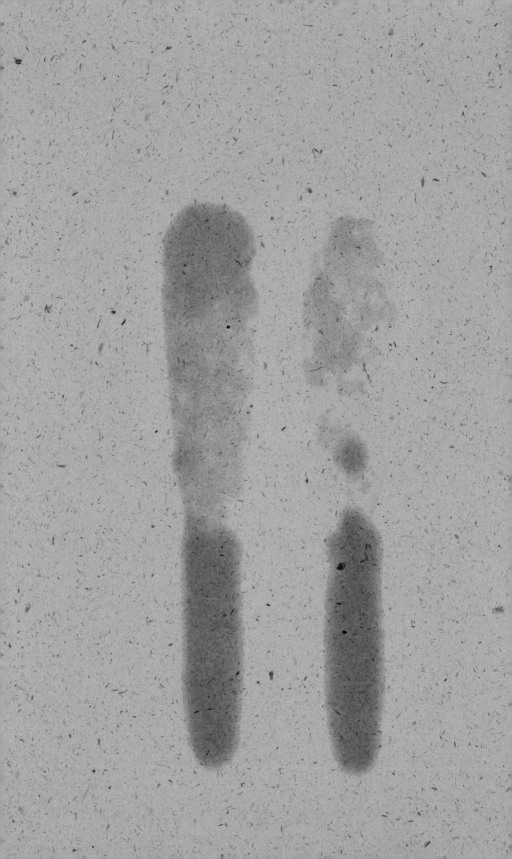

Lorenzo Magalotti
at the Court
of Charles II
His *Relazione d'Inghilterra* of 1668

W. E. Knowles Middleton, editor and translator

In the late 1660s the English court received a visitor from Florence—Lorenzo Magalotti, an intelligent, sensitive writer and diplomat with a passion for observation and description. Magalotti had come from a state governed by an absolute grand duke to a kingdom engaged in a fierce struggle for political liberty, and from a society in which the sexual behaviour of women was closely controlled by law and custom, to one of unexampled licentiousness among the upper classes. This cultural shock produced fascinating portraits by Magalotti of Charles II and his court, accounts of their amorous intrigues, and percipient if sometimes biased observations on politics. There is also a substantially accurate account of the armed forces of the kingdom, and a good deal about its intellectual and artistic life.

W. E. Knowles Middleton has provided a clear and elegant translation of this document, along with an informative introduction and supplementary notes.

W. E. Knowles Middleton was associated with the National Research Council from 1946 until 1963. He is the author of The History of the Barometer, The Experimenters: A Study of the Accademia del Cimento, *and* Physics at the National Research Council of Canada, 1929-1952 *(WLU Press, 1979). He has received honorary degrees from Boston University and McGill University.*

Lorenzo Magalotti
at the Court
of Charles II
His *Relazione d'Inghilterra* of 1668

Lorenzo Magalotti
at the Court
of Charles II

His *Relazione d'Inghilterra* of 1668

W. E. Knowles Middleton, editor & translator

Wilfrid Laurier University Press

Canadian Cataloguing in Publication Data

Magalotti, Lorenzo, conte, 1637-1712.
  Lorenzo Magalotti at the court of Charles II

Translation of Relazione d'Inghilterra.
Includes index.
ISBN 0-88920-095-5 bd.

1. Great Britain — Politics and government — 1660-
1688.   2. England — Description and travel — 1601-
1700.   3. Great Britain — Court and courtiers — 17th
century.   I. Middleton, William E. Knowles, 1902-
II. Title.

DA448.M3413   941.06'6   C80-094734-7

Copyright © 1980
WILFRID LAURIER UNIVERSITY PRESS
Waterloo, Ontario, Canada   N2L 3C5

80 81 82 83 4 3 2 1

CONTENTS

ACKNOWLEDGMENTS

The research necessary for the writing of this introduction and the notes was supported by a grant from the Canada Council, which is gratefully acknowledged.

This book has been published with the help of a grant from the Canadian Federation for the Humanities, using funds provided by the Social Sciences and Humanities Research Council of Canada.

Professor Anna Maria Crinò very kindly volunteered to read my translation and made a number of suggestions, some of which saved me from misinterpretations.

I also have to thank Professors Harriet Kirkley and Murray Tolmie of the University of British Columbia for reading the typescript and suggesting amendments, especially to the notes.

Finally I must acknowledge the never-failing co-operation of my wife, who typed the entire manuscript twice and provided the sort of detailed criticism and general encouragement that I have expected and received for many years.

ABBREVIATIONS FOR ARCHIVES, LIBRARIES, AND WORKS OF REFERENCE

ASF   Archivio di Stato, Florence

BNCF   Biblioteca Nazionale Centrale, Florence.

Burnet   Gilbert Burnet, *A History of My Own Time*. I have used the edition edited by Osmund Airy, 2 vols. (Oxford, 1897 and 1900).

CP   G. E. C[ockayne], *The Complete Peerage*, new edition by V. Gibbs and others, 12 vols. (London, 1910–1959).

DNB   *Dictionary of National Biography*.

Ediz. crit.   Lorenzo Magalotti, *Relazioni d'Inghilterra 1668 e 1688, edizione critica di editi e inediti,* a cura di Anna Maria Crinò (Firenze: Olschki, 1972).

Wood   Anthony à Wood, *Athenae oxonienses,* 2 vols. (London, 1691–1692).

Fulton   John Farquhar Fulton, *A Bibliography of the Honourable Robert Boyle . . . Second Edition* (Oxford, 1961).

INTRODUCTION

Lorenzo Magalotti was born in Rome to a noble Florentine family on December 13, 1637 of Orazio Magalotti and Francesca Venturi. His mother, a remarkably intelligent woman, saw to it that he was carefully educated, at first at home, but from the age of thirteen at the Collegio Romano, where he had excellent teachers and completed courses in philosophy and humane letters. Later he went to the University of Pisa and at first tried the study of law, a discipline that he abandoned after sixteen weeks. His stay at Pisa coincided with the tenure of Marcello Malpighi and Giovanni Alfonso Borelli, and it is believed that the young man learned some anatomy from the former and a good deal of physics from the latter. From Vincenzio Viviani, the Superintendent of Rivers for the Grand Duke Ferdinando II in Florence, he learned more physics and some mathematics, and although we may question whether he had any real mathematical ability, he must have been fairly well grounded in the science of the time when on May 20, 1660 he replaced Alessandro Segni as secretary of the scientific *Accademia del Cimento* set up by the Grand Duke Ferdinand II and his brother Leopold de' Medici.[1]

At this time Magalotti was working diligently to perfect his style in the Tuscan language—he had been brought up at Rome—and it is said that he memorized the whole of Boccaccio's *Decameron*. His first literary work, the *Saggi di naturali esperienze fatte nell'Accademia del Cimento* (1667), published anonymously under his title as secretary, shows the effect of this concentration on old models. For various reasons this book was delayed for at least five years after the material for it was available. Even before the publication of this work the *Accademia del Cimento* had ceased to exist, and indeed when the book appeared Magalotti and another

---

[1] This academy is treated at length in W. E. K. Middleton, *The Experimenters: A Study of the Accademia del Cimento* (Baltimore, 1971).

1

young nobleman, Paolo Falconieri, were on a journey through much of Europe that took them nearly a year. By this time Magalotti was in the service of the Grand Prince Cosimo, who on the death of his father, Ferdinando II, on May 24, 1670 became the Grand Duke Cosimo III. Magalotti served Cosimo in many posts for most of the rest of his life, largely in the capacity of a diplomatist.

For such employment he had superb qualifications. Apart from being very handsome, he rode and danced well, so that "he really seemed born for the court." He had a refined taste in the arts, especially architecture and painting, but above all he had almost miraculous powers of observation and the ability to sense the gist of complicated negotiations and to form mental pictures of places and people, and to write down what he learned in a clear and interesting style, as will indeed become evident to readers of the present work. His great ability in this was at once appreciated by Prince Cosimo, who when a young man had a remarkable range of interests. Magalotti arrived in Venice on July 16, 1667, and on the 23rd he was able to write the Prince a thirteen-page letter packed with political news, followed by another letter of eleven pages on the 26th. On the 30th the Prince wrote to Magalotti from Florence:

If the few steps that you have taken outside of Tuscany provide you with the material to furnish me with such a fine collection of delightful and beautiful items of news, how will it be when you discover the provinces of the north? You have certainly made a great sacrifice of sleep and of your pleasures for the sake of my tastes, for I see that you have been at pains to favour them with attention and the labours of your pen, not without much inconvenience, also overcoming the lack of time and of comfort that always distresses travellers.[2]

The subsequent career of this intelligent but restless man was varied.[3] For a number of years he travelled a great deal, visiting most of the countries of Europe. From 1675 to 1678 he was the Tuscan ambassador at the imperial court in Vienna. He became a councillor of state. For a brief period in 1691 he entered an Oratorian monastery, but it took him only a few months to realize that the religious life was not for him. By turns he became "an art connoisseur, a lexicographer, a poet, and a literary critic."[4] He

---

[2] *ASF*, Med d. Pr. 1572, 736r.

[3] An adequate biography of Magalotti is still needed.

[4] Eric Cochrane, *Florence in the Forgotten Centuries* (Chicago, 1973), p. 275. Part 4 of this book is centred around the life of Magalotti.

lived quietly and comfortably in his villa at Lonchio until his death on March 2, 1712.

The sojourn in England of which Magalotti's report is presented here formed part of his first journey outside of Italy, made in company with Paolo Falconieri, another young patrician at the Tuscan court, known only for a few lyrical verses but probably excellent company. The reason for the journey, who suggested it, and even the exact date on which it began are not known, although the material for answers to such questions may well be in the Archivio di Stato in Florence. One may deduce from the tone of his correspondence[5] that at this time Magalotti was to all intents and purposes in the service of the Grand Prince Cosimo, who himself started a journey round Europe three months later. Magalotti did not simply prepare the way for the Prince (although he did make some arrangements for Cosimo's travel to Vienna)[6] because they did not go to the same places. Nevertheless he wrote long descriptions of the courts of Munich and Vienna to the Prince, as well as extensive budgets of news from Venice. It must be remembered that in the seventeenth century Venice was almost as "foreign" a capital to Magalotti in the political sense as London or Paris.

We do know that he arrived in Venice on July 16, 1667, for he at once wrote to the Prince to tell him so.[7] Paolo Falconieri joined him there on the 22nd,[8] as he informed Cosimo's secretary, Appollonio Bassetti. We may guess that Magalotti left Florence during the first week of July, for among his accounts[9] there are an unusual number of tradesmen's receipts dated July 2nd and 3rd, 1667, and none for some time thereafter.

The two noblemen left Venice on July 28[10] after being delayed by a violent storm, which reminds us that Venice was then really surrounded by the sea. We next hear from Magalotti at Augsburg, from where he wrote both to Cosimo[11] and to Viviani[12]

---

[5] I have been able to identify sixty-five letters pertinent to this journey between Magalotti's departure from Florence and his arrival in Paris after his stay in England. I have published forty-seven of these in *Studi secenteschi*, 20 (1980), 123−202.

[6] *ASF*, Med. d. Pr. 1572, 727r.

[7] Ibid., 717r.

[8] Ibid., 1142r–1143v.

[9] *ASF*, Carte Magalotti 184.

[10] Magalotti to Cosimo, July 27, 1667. *ASF*., Med. d. Pr. 1572, 734r. They were to leave at daybreak next day.

[11] *ASF*, Med. d. Pr. 4489, 354r–359r.

[12] Florence, *Biblioteca Riccardiana*, MS Ricc. 2487, 83r–84r.

on August 10. In his letter to the Prince he describes the city of Trento and the Archduke's court at Innsbruck; the one to his great friend Viviani, who was an avid collector, is largely about books. These two letters are excellent examples of his epistolary styles— the descriptive to the Prince, the intimate to Viviani. He informs both his correspondents that he is leaving the following day for Vienna by way of Neuburg, Ingolstadt, Ratisbon [Regensburg], and from there down the Danube. He and Falconieri were in Ratisbon on the 14th[13] and in Vienna a week later,[14] where he wrote the Prince a seventeen-page letter including an enthusiastic description of Munich and its court—a result of only two days' stay.

They departed from Vienna on September 30, after enjoying the imperial court. I have found fourteen letters between Vienna and Florence (or Artimino, the Grand Duke's summer retreat) during that period, which included a nine-day tour in Hungary, duly described on September 25.[15] Magalotti also sent pen portraits[16] of the chief people at the court, other than the sovereigns. All this activity drew thanks from Cosimo on October 1 and 8, with an expression of worry that Magalotti might be working too hard.[17]

From Prague on October 8 Cosimo was told that they had decided to forego an excursion to Dresden. They planned to go by way of Nuremberg to Frankfort and Mainz, down the Rhine to Strasbourg, thence to Nancy, Commercy (to see Cardinal de Retz), Verdun, Metz, Thionville, Luxembourg, Liège, Cologne, and down the Rhine again to Wesel, Cleves, Utrecht, and Amsterdam.[18] Cosimo, who had meanwhile started on his own journey, answered this from Innsbruck on November 12.[19] He was afraid that Magalotti's idea of seeing the Rhine and the Moselle would "receive some alterations because of the outbreaks of plague that are affecting those parts." He hoped to meet the two travellers in Holland.

---

[13] Magalotti to Cosimo, August 14, 1667. *ASF, Med. d. Pr.* 4489, 360r–361r.
[14] Ibid., August 21, 362r–370r.
[15] Ibid., 382r–387r.
[16] Ibid., 396r–400v.
[17] Ibid., 401r and 402r.
[18] Ibid., 405r–407v.
[19] Cosimo to Magalotti, ibid., 415r–v.

We do not know how much of their itinerary was carried out; only that they were in Cologne on November 5[20] and that they arrived in Amsterdam on the 12th,[21] finding three letters from the Prince. One of these, which I have not found, must have contained an order to wait for Cosimo's party in the Low Countries, and this they did, making forays to The Hague,[22] Breda, Antwerp,[23] and other places.

The letter that Magalotti wrote to Cardinal Leopold from Antwerp gives us an indication that he was anxious— "unspeakably curious"—to know what people were thinking about the *Saggi di naturali esperienze,* on which he had worked so long and hard. He was also worried about the copies that were destined for England, to be presented to the King and the Royal Society, for he had written from The Hague[24] to say that he would not be in England until spring. He was concerned about how Charles II would receive him, for he had been told—no doubt by some disgruntled refugee—that the King always referred to the Fellows of the Royal Society as his fools![25]

By the middle of January Magalotti and Falconieri were quite happy in Brussels, as is clear from a charming letter to Cardinal Leopold dated January 21, 1668.[26] It transpires from this that they expected to go to Paris to be in time for the last of the carnival. Magalotti also informed the Cardinal that he was in love, so much so that he did not know whether he would go back to Italy after he had been to France and England, or to Brussels to take a wife. There is no indication that this infatuation lasted, and on February 4 Magalotti wrote again to the Cardinal[27] rather less boisterously. They had misread the calendar by about three weeks, as Cosimo's physician, Andrea Moneglia, had pointed out to them.[28] There

---

[20] Magalotti to Cosimo, November 5, 1667. *ASF, Med. d. Pr.* 4489, 404r.

[21] Magalotti to Cosimo, November 18, 1667. *Med. d. Pr.* 4260, 133r–v.

[22] Magalotti to Francesco Redi, December 15, 1667. *Biblioteca Medicea Laurenziana,* MS Redi 206, 53r–56r.

[23] Magalotti to Cardinal Leopold, January 6, 1668. *BNCF,* Gal. 278, 119r–120v. Published, but with errors and omissions, by A. Fabroni in *Lettere inedite d'uomini illustri,* 2 vols. (Florence, 1773 and 1775), I, pp. 295–98.

[24] I have not found this letter.

[25] See W. E. K. Middleton, *Notes and Records of the Royal Society,* 32 (1977), 13–16.

[26] *ASF,* Carte Magalotti 190, inserto 10, letter 3.

[27] Ibid., letter 4.

[28] Easter day was on April 1 (N.S.) in 1668, Ash Wednesday on February 14.

was not nearly enough time to get to Paris for the carnival, and so they had decided to visit England before going to France. This again raised the question of the books for the King and the Society:

The day before yesterday I wrote to Colonel Guasconi[29] about this, asking him to put off the execution of the orders that he may receive from Your Highness in the meantime regarding the presentation of the two books that have been sent to him, because this will have been done on the assumption that I should not be coming to London before the beginning of spring. I thought I had enough reason to take this action, for I was certain that Your Highness' intentions has always been to give me the opportunity to have this extra introduction to the king, and that it could not be altered in any way except by the delay in my arrival at that court.

He had also written to the Tuscan Resident in Paris, asking him to send on letters.

The Cardinal, who was very busy with his preparations to visit Rome—he had been promoted only on December 12, 1667—answered five of Magalotti's letters from Pisa on February 24, 1668.[30] He would write to Guasconi himself about the books. He assured Magalotti that the *Saggi* "is being applauded and esteemed everywhere, and you should receive the praise that is indeed due to your merit." We may wonder if Leopold really took at their face value the fulsome letters that he was receiving from those to whom he had sent the book.[31] He smiled an avuncular smile at the young man's amatory enthusiasm: "I am glad that your stay in Brussels has been so satisfactory on account of the gallant entertainments of the ladies, and in fact you will certainly have acknowledged that our part of the world produces people of colder blood than many others." As far as Paris was concerned, he was sure that Magalotti would enjoy it when he got there, even if he did miss the carnival.

Long before Magalotti received this letter he and Falconieri had arrived in London, which they reached on February 8/18

---

[29] Sir Bernard Gascoigne (1614–1687), originally Bernardino Guasconi, a Florentine who had fought valiantly for Charles I, and was admitted to English citizenship and knighted by Charles II in 1661. In 1667 he had been made a Fellow of the Royal Society. It seems that he assisted every Italian of note who came to England at this time. Magalotti's letter to Gascoigne was actually written on January 31. It is in Paris at the Bibliothèque Nationale, fonds ital. 2035, 269r–270r, and was printed by C. Delcorno in *Studi Secenteschi,* 7 (1966), 141–42.

[30] *ASF,* Carte Magalotti 190, 78r–79r.

[31] Many of these are in *BNCF,* Gal. 314.

1667/8.[32] It is very unfortunate that no diary exists (or at least none has been discovered) that would enable us to follow their motions day by day and in particular to find out to whom Magalotti had been talking, so that we might guess intelligently at the sources of some of the surprising information that he provided in his report. We have a very full diary of a visit made ten months later by two other Florentines, Marchese Francesco Riccardi and Alessandro Segni, which does tempt one to make guesses about this.[33] We have only a few isolated pieces of information about what Magalotti was doing, chiefly in the letters of Henry Oldenburg,[34] the minutes of the Royal Society,[35] and of course Magalotti's own letters. Much of this information was presented forty years ago by R. D. Waller,[36] although his work can now be extended somewhat.

Magalotti and Falconieri were out walking with Sir Bernard Gascoigne on February 10 when they happened to meet Oldenburg, the secretary of the Royal Society, who was introduced to them and learned that they intended to present a copy of "the Florentine experiments" to the Society.[37] It is significant that although Oldenburg told Robert Boyle that Gascoigne "brought us together," he had "not yet heard" the name of the other "Florentine virtuoso." As it cannot be believed that Sir Bernard would not have introduced both Magalotti and Falconieri, we must suppose that Magalotti was much the more impressive of the

---

[32] The matter of dating demands a note. From 1583 to 1752 the British Isles continued to use the old Julian calendar, which in 1668 was ten days behind the revised one used in most of Europe. At the same time the year was considered to begin on March 25 both in England and in Florence (though not elsewhere except in ecclesiastical circles); so that, e.g., the date of the travellers' arrival in London would be written February 8, 1667/8 by someone in England, and February 18, 1667 *ab Inc.* [*arnazione*] by a Florentine. A Parisian would have written it February 18, 1668. But in England people with Continental correspondents would generally use the form February 8/18, 1667/8. In what follows I shall use the Old Style dates, referring to the year as 1667/8 until after March 25 O.S.

[33] I hope to publish this diary, which is in the *Biblioteca Riccardiana,* MS Ricc. 2298.

[34] *The Correspondence of Henry Oldenburg,* ed. & transl. by A. Rupert Hall and Marie Boas Hall (Madison & Milwaukee), [in progress], vols. 3 and 4.

[35] Thomas Birch, *History of the Royal Society,* 4 vols. (London, 1756–1757).

[36] R. D. Waller, *Italian Studies,* 1 (1937), 49–66.

[37] *Oldenburg Corr.,* 4, 169–71. (Oldenburg to Robert Boyle, February 11, 1667/8.)

two. The copies of the book had still not arrived, so that Magalotti need not have worried about having been forestalled.

Three days later, as he informed Cardinal Leopold, he turned up at the usual Thursday meeting of the Society, but stopped at the door: "having found out that entry was not permitted to a simple passer-by, I did not want to get a place for myself as a scholar, firstly because I am not one, and secondly because even if I were I should not consider it the most advantageous character for getting into courts."[38]

The Florentines nevertheless visited Oldenburg, who returned their visit on Sunday, February 23, as he told Boyle two days later. They were supposed to leave for Oxford on that day, mainly to visit Boyle, but also to meet the mathematician John Wallis and Christopher Wren.[39] For some reason this visit had to be postponed until March 1, and in the meantime they had been to two meetings of the Society. The first, on February 20, was described at some length in a very interesting letter to Leopold written the next day.[40] Magalotti said that the President, Lord Brouncker, was absent, but in fact they came very late, after his departure, as Oldenburg noted in a letter to Boyle.[41] Nevertheless Magalotti described one or two things of which Oldenburg's minutes make no mention.[42] We have no letter to Leopold referring to the meeting on February 27, although the minutes record the presence of the Italians.[43] We have a letter written two days later to Vincenzio Viviani,[44] but it is remarkable that Magalotti made no reference to the meeting, or indeed to the Society itself.

The visit to Boyle was a great success; Magalotti spent ten hours with him in two days and a half, as he told Leopold on March 13.[45] In Oxford they also went to see John Wallis[46] and apparently

---

[38] *BNCF*, MS Gal. 278, 145r–146r. Much of this letter was printed by Waller, *Italian Studies*, 1, 52–53.

[39] *Oldenburg Corr.*, 2, 206.

[40] *BNCF*, Gal. 278, 151r–152v. Printed by Fabroni, *Lettre inedite*, I, pp. 298–301; translated by Waller, *Italian Studies*, 1, 53–55.

[41] *Oldenburg Corr.*, 2, 206.

[42] See note 56, p. 152 below.

[43] Birch, *History*, 2, 252–54.

[44] *Biblioteca Riccardiana*, MS Ricc. 2487, 92r.

[45] *BNCF*, Gal. 278, 154r–155r. Fabroni, 1, 301–303. Translated by Waller, *Italian Studies*, 57–58 and 59–60.

[46] Wallis to Grand Duke Cosimo, November 9, 1670. *BNCF*, MS Gal. 285, 56r–v (in Latin).

the antiquary Anthony Wood.[47] This letter also contains an account of the presentation to the Royal Society of the copy of the *Saggi di naturali esperienze* that is still in its library. This was on March 12.[48] On March 25 Magalotti was able to present a copy, "bound as richly as possible," to the King.[49] On April 6 the two Florentines left Dover for Calais.

We know more about Magalotti's stay in Paris, from his arrival on April 23, 1668 (N.S.) until July 5, because he wrote a sort of diary in the form of frequent letters, presumably to Cosimo's secretary, Appollonio Bassetti.[50] He was still in Paris with Falconieri on July 20, when he wrote to Viviani,[51] but shortly afterwards they were ordered by the Grand Duke Ferdinando to come back to Florence in order to accompany Prince Cosimo on another and more extensive journey that was to take them to Spain, to Portugal, to the coast of Ireland, to England, to Holland, and to France. The official account of these travels, due in part to the Marchese Filippo Corsini and in part to Magalotti, is in various manuscripts in Florence. The part dealing with England was translated into English anonymously and published in 1821 by J. Mawman.[52] The Italian text has been published with great erudition by Anna Maria Crinò.[53] We shall not here be concerned with this second voyage except by way of occasional comments in the notes.

It is, however, important to consider the status of the Italian texts on which the present translation depends.

The only complete manuscript version of the *Relazione d'Inghilterra* is in the Archivio di Stato at Florence.[54] This is the work of some unknown copyist, and while it is very easy to read, it is full

---

[47] Wood does not mention this visit in his *Fasti*, but there is a letter from Lorenzo Panciatichi to Magalotti dated from London on May 30, 1671 in Magalotti's *Lettere familiari*, 2 vols. (Florence, 1769), 2, 21–23. It contains the phrase "Wood, Boyle, etc. are all very fond (*innamorati*) of you."

[48] Birch, *History*, 2, 256.

[49] *BNCF*, Gal. 278, 167r–168r. Printed by Waller, *Italian Studies*, 1, 60–61.

[50] These have been published by Walter Moretti in Lorenzo Magalotti, *Relazioni di Viaggio in Inghilterra, Francia, e Svezia* (Bari: Laterza, 1968).

[51] *Biblioteca Riccardiana*, MS Ricc. 2487, 100r–101r.

[52] *Travels of Cosimo the Third, Grand Duke of Tuscany, Through England, During the Reign of King Charles the Second (1669)*, etc. (London, 1821).

[53] *Un principe di Toscana in Inghilterra e in Irlanda nel 1669* (Roma: Edizioni di Storia e Letteratura, 1968).

[54] *ASF*, Carte Strozziane, Series 1, no. 299, fol. 3r–116v.

of errors in orthography, highly aberrant spellings of English proper names, lacunae, and a few passages that seem entirely garbled. It is remarkable that no more than fragments of it were published in Italian until 1968, when Walter Moretti provided a version in the work already mentioned.[55] This was derived almost entirely from the above manuscript, with the addition of a little information from file number 267 in the Archivio Venturi-Ginori at Florence. Moretti's version left much to be desired, not merely on linguistic grounds but because he was not sufficiently aware of English usage in the seventeenth century. Its shortcomings induced Professor Anna Maria Crinò, now at the University of Pisa, who for twenty years has been an authority on English-Italian relations in the *seicento*,[56] to publish another edition in 1972.[57]

Professor Crinò had the great advantage of being aware of a manuscript in the British Museum, Egerton 1703, acquired for the Museum in 1857. This manuscript contains a *Ragguaglio della corte d'Inghilterra in tempo di re Carlo II fatto dal conte Lorenzo Magalotti dell'anno 1669,* and also *Memorie attenenti al regno d'Inghilterra,* and other related documents. Miss Crinò discovered that these had been written out for the information of Jacopo Giraldi, a friend of Magalotti's who was sent to London as Tuscan ambassador in 1699.

The *Ragguaglio*[58] is derived entirely from parts of the *Relazione,* and the parts that were omitted would certainly have been of no use to an ambassador thirty years later. On the other hand, the pen-portraits of the great men of the court were completely out of date, most of them being dead. However this may be, the existence of ms. Egerton 1703 not only served to remove any doubts lingering in the minds of some scholars that Magalotti really was the author of the *Relazione* of 1667/8, but in combination with Magalotti's holograph notes in Venturi-Ginori 267, made it possible for Professor Crinò to establish a comprehensible text in spite of the serious defects of the Strozzi manuscript. She has even decoded a few passages in cipher. She has also gone to great trouble to restore the orthography to the forms that Magalotti was in the habit of using, although this will of course not be apparent to readers of the following translation.

---

[55] Note 50.

[56] Cf. her *Fatti e figure del seicento anglo-toscano* (Florence: Olschki, 1957).

[57] Lorenzo Magalotti, *Relazioni d'Inghilterra 1668 e 1688, edizione critica di editi e inediti a cura di Anna Maria Crinò* (Firenze: Olschki, 1972).

[58] It is printed after the *Relazione* by Miss Crinò (pp. 163–211).

The writer obtained a microfilm of the Strozzi manuscript and began translating it while waiting for the Moretti and Crinò versions to arrive from Italy. The insoluble problems posed by the manuscript were not much helped by Moretti's text, which was the first to arrive, but these problems largely disappeared when Professor's Crinò's excellent edition became available.

It is worthwhile to inquire into, or at least to speculate about, Magalotti's probable sources of information while he was in England. He was well acquainted with Sir Bernard Gascoigne, and indeed had been with him only two days after his arrival, as we have seen. He had a letter of recommendation to the permanent Tuscan representative in London, Giovanni Salvetti Antelminelli, but Magalotti does not seem to have presented it for about a fortnight. Nor does Salvetti seem to have been notified that he was coming, judging by his letter of February 29, 1667/8 to the Grand Duke's secretary, Felice Marchetti:

Besides the usual dispatch of February 4 that I received from you this week, I was presented by Signor Lorenzo Magalotti with another letter of yours recommending that gentleman; and in conformity with your orders I have offered to help him in every way that he might be pleased to command me or make use of me. As I was forestalled in this matter by the kindness of Sir [Bernard] Gascoigne before I knew of the arrival of this gentleman in this city, I want to hope that both you and he will take the goodwill for the fact, and that you will not cease to favour me sometimes with your commands.[59]

The Italians that Magalotti actually mentions in the *Relazione* are far from an impressive group. The self-styled Count Carlo Ubaldini, a soldier of fortune of very doubtful reputation, would scarcely have furnished our author with any information that he could trust. There were others whom he does not name, notably three merchants called Antinori, Del Rosso, and Terriesi,[60] who

---

[59] *ASF*, Med. d. Pr. 4207 (not numbered).

"Oltre al solito dispaccio delli 4 febbraio che questa settimana ricevò da VS Illustrissima mi fu presentata dal signor Lorenzo Magalotti un'altra sua lettera in racomandazione di quel Cavaliere; et conforme al suo comando mi sono offerto di servirlo, in tutto e per tutti, che li piacesse di comandarmi, e valersene della mia persona; nel quale io essendo stato prevenuto della cortesia del Signor Cavalier Guasconi, dinanzi ch'io seppi l'arrivo di detto Cavaliere in questa città; voglio sperare che VS Illustrissima et quel Cavaliere piglieranno la buona volontà per il fatto, et che non lascierà di favorirmi alle volte delli suoi comandi."

[60] Francesco Terriesi acted as an agent for the Grand Duke and was later Consul. See Crinò, *Fatti e figure,* passim.

were the first people mentioned in the diary of Segni and Riccardi ten months later.[61] There was another called Brunetti, at whose house they met a nephew[62] of Sir John Finch, the King's Resident at Florence, and discussed the geography, history, and religions of the British Isles with him, apparently at great length.[63] At the house of the Venetian ambassador, Pietro Mocenigo, they met Henry Howard, who later became sixth Duke of Norfolk; they had several meetings with him, and went to see his "cabinet" at Arundel House. It is natural that those with whom they had the closest relations were Roman Catholics or at least sympathetic to the Roman Catholic faith, and as there were not very many of these it is reasonable to suppose that most Italian visitors of importance would meet the same group. Among these sympathetic people the French, Spanish, and Venetian ambassadors obviously stood out. I incline to the belief that much of the personal gossip that Magalotti reports was picked up from these ambassadors or people in their suites.

Information about the more prominent intellectuals may have been partly obtained from Robert Boyle during the ten hours that Magalotti spent with him, but I suspect that much more was obtained from Henry Howard. It might be supposed that the very miscellaneous list of books set down near the end of the *Relazione* represented a selection from the library of Henry Howard, but an examination of the catalogue of the collection later presented by the Duke to the Royal Society[64] shows only two correspondences, apart from the works of Robert Boyle. As there are at least twenty-five scientific and medical books that would interest the Royal Society in Magalotti's list, it is highly unlikely that the list has its origin in the library at Arundel House.

The interest of Magalotti's report lies not in its factual accuracy, which is at times lacking, but in the responses of a very intelligent young Italian suddenly confronted with a society whose values differed greatly from those of his own. Coming from a grand duchy in which the ruler was absolutely powerful, to a kingdom engaged in a struggle for political liberty must have been a shock.

---

61 MS Ricc. 2298, 4r.
62 Daniel Finch (1647–1730).
63 MS Ricc. 2298, 5r–10r.
64 *Bibliotheca Norfolciana: sive catalogus libb. manuscriptorum & impressorum . . . quos . . . Henricus Dux Norfolciae, &c. Regiae Societati . . . donavit* (London, 1681). I wish to thank Mr. Geoffrey Beard of the University of Lancaster for confronting Magalotti's list with this catalogue in the British Library.

The transition from a society in which the sexual behaviour of women was closely controlled by law and custom to one of un-exampled licentiousness among the upper classes must have been a greater one. Another phenomenon that seems to have greatly displeased him and coloured many of his character sketches is the widespread and massive peculation by officials at the time, a practice that was considered quite normal. There was undoubtedly much less of this in Tuscany, for several reasons: the country was smaller and at that time much less prosperous than England, and such action was frowned upon by the Medici grand dukes, who tacitly identified the revenues of the grand duchy with their own incomes.

It must have been a relief to Magalotti to turn to the intellec-tual and cultural aspects of English life, for which he had such a great respect that he soon acquired a reputation as an anglophile in his own country.

It remains to discuss, or rather to speculate about the cir-cumstances of the composition of the *Relazione*. A capital diffi-culty, with no solution in sight until further documents are discovered, is to find out the name of the person for whom it was intended. It cannot have been either the Grand Duke or Prince Cosimo, since in the third paragraph Magalotti uses the form *V.S.*, meaning simply "you," whereas if it had been addressed to any of the ruling family he would have been obliged to use *V.A.*, "Your Highness." I have not discovered any other use of *V.S.* in the text, nor any other form of address. Furthermore the first pages are written in a highly self-conscious and "literary" style, as if meant for publication, but by the time Magalotti gets round to describing the various courtiers he has relapsed into a matter-of-fact—though clear and graphic—manner which, incidentally, I found very much easier to translate. It is possible that by the time he had got that far he realized that much of his material was of a sort that it would not be wise for a man in his position to publish. He may, in fact, not have had a correspondent in mind at all, but have originally intended to adopt the epistolary form, a favourite literary device at that period. If he had published the *Relazione* he would undoubtedly have revised it greatly.

Although Professor Crinò has edited some holograph notes that Magalotti clearly made at the time of his visit, there is both internal and external evidence that the actual writing of the *Relazione* was done in 1669. For example, on page 53 he refers to the Dutch raid on Chatham as having taken place "two years ago."

It occurred in June, 1667. In the diary of his visit to France he states, under the date of May 15, 1668, that he and some friends were discussing a new invention of Sir Samuel Morland, "of whom," he states, "I shall speak at greater length when I come to deal with the people at that court. I have already seen this invention in London."[65] This would indicate that the *Relazione* was not yet written. Professor Crinò has given excellent reasons for supposing that it was written only after Magalotti's return from his second journey, the one in the suite of Prince Cosimo, that is to say, at the end of 1669.[66] In 1668 he had been recalled from Paris to Florence and would scarcely have had time to write it while making preparations for Cosimo's travels. There is, of course, no certainty that its composition was continuous.

Finally a word about Magalotti's state of mind at this time. For several years, as secretary of the *Accademia del Cimento,* he had had the task, which cannot have been very congenial to a young man with literary aspirations, of recording the actions of that difficult group of virtuosi. Then he began the process of writing the *Saggi* in such a way as to satisfy first the academicians as to its content, and then Cardinal Sforza Pallavicino (1607–1667) as a sort of literary consultant imposed on him by the Prince, and finally himself—a perfectionist. I have dealt elsewhere with his struggles.[67] There can be no doubt that he regarded his journey as a relief from toil, even though he worked very hard at it, as we have seen. It was even more a relief from "natural philosophy," and this explains his occasional outbursts in his letters to Cardinal Leopold about his determination not to be taken for a "philosopher."[68] Leopold, who was a wise man and genuinely fond of Magalotti, cannot have taken these declarations very seriously.

Cochrane[69] does not believe that Magalotti was very highly sexed, although he obviously enjoyed the company of attractive women. His occasional searches for sexual gratification—the description of a brothel seems entirely circumstantial—were no more than was expected of healthy young men at the time. Somewhat less healthy, we may feel, is his obvious delight in retailing

---

[65] Moretti, *Relazioni,* p. 174. "di cui trattando dei soggetti di quella corte parlerò piu diffusamente a suo tempo. Quest'invenzione l'avevo già veduta a Londra."

[66] *Ediz. crit.*, p. 8.

[67] In Chapter 4 of reference 1.

[68] See pp. 8 and 62.

[69] Reference 4.

malicious gossip, of which there was plenty at the court of St. James. Much too much of this appears in the *Relazione*. I think that we may take it that he was at rather a loose end, between the "scientific" portion of his career and his later diplomatic vocation.

There is nothing to be gained by insisting on Magalotti's many errors of fact and interpretation, some of which I have pointed out in the notes. It is more appropriate to wonder at the very large amount of fairly accurate information about people and offices, troops, and ships that he garnered in the short space of fifty-nine days,[70] not to mention the weekly diplomatic reports, some of them partly in cipher, that he wrote in his own hand to Appollonio Bassetti, the Prince's secretary.[71] A twentieth-century journalist with a tape recorder might have done no more and not been idle. For me at least the *Relazione* is the work of a young man who might have made a superb historian if only he had had any desire to do so. It is a pity that he did not.

---

[70] As much or possibly all of the *Relazione* was not written until after his visit in 1669 in the suite of Prince Cosimo, some of his information may have been gathered on this second visit. This suspicion applies particularly to the "genealogical" statements on pp. 114 to 120.

[71] These are in *ASF*, Med. d. Princ., filze 4240, 4260, and 4289.

THE TEXT

An Account of England in the Year 1667 – 68

To form a sure judgment of the present position of England is impossible to a man just arrived and acquainted with no one at the court,[1] so that unless he remains there a very long time, it pays him better to disregard the more fundamental principles that rule the actions of that government, and content himself with information concerning the personal characters of the most noteworthy ministers and other people. Since if I wish to fix on the former object, the space of a few weeks is not enough to get beyond the surface of things, and it nevertheless demands hearing so many people, and asking so many questions, that no time is left to consider the second. Although this latter course does not lead us to a deep understanding of this intricate system, nevertheless it makes it easier to find out the truth about it, and serves to provide a confused outline of the present state of the kingdom, and the private affairs of the court, not without giving some slight idea of the vicissitudes to which both are subject.

This difficulty of understanding what arts and mechanisms move this perturbed and disorderly machine results not so much from the disadvantages of a foreigner with no help but his own curiosity, as from the perpetual changeableness with which everything is directed and governed. From this it follows that even if one tries hard to understand the necessary rules, they change before

---

[1] This is slightly disingenuous, for Magalotti knew Sir Bernard Gasciogne, and indeed had written to him regarding his visit from Brussels on January 31, 1668. See C. Delcorno, *Studi Secenteschi,* 7 (1966), 141–42. See also my introduction, p. 6 above.

one can finish getting them into one's head. Thus even though a person considers himself an industrious inquirer he very soon becomes aware that it is something already belonging to the past, and that his knowledge is like that of one who manages to find out what o'clock it is, when the time denoted by that hour is already past. In the short time that I remained at this court I did my best to converse with people of various ranks, with the sole precaution of choosing those who, because of their experience, profession, or calling, or their dispassionate minds, I thought might be the best informed or the most sincere. However, either truth in England is different from itself or it is not clear to anybody, so much disagreement have I found in their opinions of the present state of affairs, and inconsistencies in their judgments about the future.

Nevertheless in order not to leave the portraits of the people whom I am about to paint for you on the bare background of the canvas, I shall do as those painters do, who to provide some emphasis furnish nearby a view of a room or a landscape, as much as needful to bring all out clearly. But I declare that to the extent that I have to complete and recover the finest lineaments of faces, to that extent I must needs leave all the rest sketched in, or imperfect.

The Present Constitution of England

In his kingdom the King of England is not what kings and princes usually are in their dominions. Nor indeed is he what he has been believed to be, even by those who are very knowledgeable about that monarchy. For his subjects he is nothing but the source of honour and of favours, although by the fundamental laws of the realm the title of Monarch is not apparently given him with such great reservation, but makes him the arbiter of peace and war and leaves him all the authority to decide for himself, and not to let others choose what he does not want. Nevertheless in arbitrating peace and war he is constrained by a stronger law (everything depends on the force of circumstances) to control with such discerning shrewdness the use of this sovereignty of his, that it cannot be said that it resides entirely in him. He is at least constrained to moderate it with the bridle of his own circumspection, without ever being able to abandon the control of it to the needs of self-interest or the transports of passion.

I think that two things have brought the King into his present condition: the supreme authority divided too equally between the King and his subjects, and the change of religion. The first, altering by its own inconsistency the ancient government of the realm, turned it so much in favour of the King that to make sure of possessing it, he came with a remedy so extreme as to make it become the seed of new evil. This insensibly increased, and returned to the first state of that dangerous equilibrium of authority between King and subjects, from which one could fear every day that it would reach the point where the usual inconsistency of this government would begin to operate; but with this difference, that whereas in the first conflict religion fought on the King's side, in this one it will be against him. Where previously the King won, and exterminated his enemies while pretending to help them, so that they had no thought of defence until they were quite thrown down, now he will have to triumph with blood and arms. But the arms have to be provided him by his enemies themselves, or else he has to expect them from chance events as a reward for wise conduct. And that this is true is shown by the fact that the riches, the popularity, and the strength of the nobles, who had deposed kings before, so greatly frightened Henry VII, who without illusions recognized the weakness of his right to the crown,[2] that in order to secure it for himself he was obliged to disunite the nobles and destroy them. As I have said, he succeeded in doing this with the appearance of conferring a benefit, for, seeing the extreme subjection in which the nobles found themselves, and considering the insupportable weight of the excessive debts, impossible to satisfy by advances on the annual levies, he rejected the laws against misappropriation of funds and freed himself from them under the appearance of paternal affection. At the same time, by impoverishing the most powerful (some being exhausted by the payments, some because of the division of families by the equal distribution of goods freed from the fetters of primogeniture) he dispelled all the shadows of his fears, and defended himself with the addition of the authority taken from the nobles, the existence of which rendered him insecure because it was too uniformly distributed.

Since this property was coming little by little into the hands of another circle of people of a lower class, who by way of commerce had accumulated a great deal of money, some spirit of ambition began to awake in them, with the result that in later times King James, who had come from Scotland new to the realm and a stranger, deemed that he could not better make himself secure

---

[2] He had usurped the throne of Richard III.

than by forming a new party depending on him. In this way, finding great riches among the common people, firmly established by the purchase of the ancient estates of the nobles, and considering them able to support with sufficient splendour the dignities that he was going to give them, he began to raise many of them to the highest ranks in the kingdom, and to amplify the privileges, already grown too large, of the House of Commons, to the ever greater discredit of the House of Lords, now reduced to being a majestic court of supreme justice, but in what concerns the important decisions about the affairs of the kingdom, despoiled of every ornament of credit or authority.

That is how this expedient, which from the first consisted in the abasement of the nobles, finally became the seed of new evil, while by slow and insensible increments the authority that had all fallen into the hands of the King continually went on increasing in a new popular party which, returned once more to equilibrium, not only did to the King what he had done to the nobility in abasing it, but destroyed his power, and gave rise to the beginning of a republic. Even if this died in infancy, it was because those who ought to have nourished it by their own moderation and disinterest have been the first to crush it and make room once more for the King. If he had firmly held the authority that fell at first into his hands in the fluctuating state of England, there is no doubt that at present he also could be considered as being like other princes in their states. But the malicious self-interest of others advised him to act in such a way that this authority has gradually come to be divided again, and today it is so near that perilous equality that (as I have said) the results usually produced by this may come once again. While King and Parliament are so necessary to each other, and while each party is averse to giving the other the authority that it requires in order to operate efficiently according to its urgent needs, it is impossible that they should not make themselves intolerable to each other, and that both should not think of freeing themselves forever from such a necessary and troublesome subjection.

When this will happen is very uncertain, and it is extremely uncertain how things will turn out and which party will reap the advantage, which in the past has changed day by day, at one time favouring the King against his nobles and at another the people against the King. This part of my first argument is also certainly infallible, that this time the King will not have religion in his favour as Henry VII had, and that the party that he has to overcome is not one to be defeated, like the earlier one, by means of apparent benefits. He will have to do it with armed force; and as this must have the support of money, with which he is entirely unprovided, he must needs get it from his enemies or else, renewing all the principles of his past conduct, must put himself into a position to profit from the favours of fortune without their help, whenever it pleases her to open roads to him which up to now have been closed. And we shall see that this is true if the two most stable foundations of the monarchy are considered, for they will both be found weak and feeble.

The nobility, as I have said, are poor, weak, and destitute of authority. Religion, although that which is professed in the kingdom accords better than any other except the Catholic with the maintenance of the King because of the subordination of the bishops, must nevertheless be considered an imaginary thing, existing in outward show and ostentation. As for the conduct of the bishops, it is the most scandalous and abhorred in the whole country.[3] Their principles are avarice, sordid love of money, forgetting their pastoral offices, eager care for their domestic affairs, pomp, pride, hypocrisy, debauchery, lasciviousness, favouring those of the party opposing their religion and their very existence, and above all reserving to themselves the property of their churches, in land as well as in what may serve for the ordinary use of their houses, and taking from what remains all the money they find. This they turn into freeholds in order to reap the profits that these will yield many years after their deaths, to the very great detriment of church property and of those who succeed to the episcopate after them. What is more, some among them hold different views about the articles of their religion, which therefore becomes an incomprehensible cabal, so that the beliefs that agree best with the doctrine of the bishop most in favour with the King gradually prevail. Hatred of the bishops increases because people see how in the King's frequent need of money, all the taxes are placed on the laity, always leaving the estates of the ecclesiastics, in one way or another, unharmed.

---

[3] It is interesting that in 1666 Gilbert Burnet (1643–1715), although only twenty-three, wrote a memorial to the Scottish bishops accusing them of just the things that Magalotti mentions (Burnet, *History of My Own Time*, 2 vols. [Oxford: 1897 and 1900], vol. 1, p. 177). It is known that Magalotti read the *Relation d'un voyage en Angleterre* (Paris, 1664) of Samuel de Sorbière, who made similar charges.

All these things excite in the Protestants,[4] together with contempt for their superiors, a beastly and licentious life, and a confusion of principles and dogmas and opinions that in the lower classes appears as superstition, in the nobility as atheism.[5]

The erection of altars, the clerical habits, the music, the organs, the prayers, very like those of the Church of Rome, the litanies (although without the invocation of the saints), and the formality of the ceremonies, are all the strong points of this religion, and at the same time give to its enemies, who are also those of the King, and to the friends of novelties and sedition, the strongest argument in persuading the people of the designs of the bishops to lead England back under the yoke of Rome and into the errors of the old Roman superstition.

In this way they will procure the extermination of the Anglican reform and put the scythe to the roots of the monarchy. This could be done because the avaricious and proud spirit of the nation, in that brief period of liberty, came to know what the country might be without the King. Remembering that they conquered France with only the forces of the kingdom itself, they cannot bear having lost so much to Holland in a peace that followed a war in which they won more battles than their enemies did, and that in a time when, from the increase in commerce, they might be said to have been assisted by the forces of Asia and America, notwithstanding the abundance of treasure in the King's exchequer, into which has come more money from the realm in these eight years since his return than in the times of all his predecessors.

By a greater misfortune it chances that the Presbyterian party is credited with having some religion, so that ignorant people believe them. As most of that party are intelligent, deceitful, and astute, they have too great an advantage over those who abandon themselves to drunkenness and pleasures and make themselves incapable of defending themselves against their cunning. And so it happens that although Parliament is mostly composd of Protestants, yet that small party of secret Presbyterians sometimes manages to be the strongest.

---

[4] By "Protestants," Magalotti means the Church of England, here and elsewhere.

[5] The nobility were not philosophical atheists, but many were libertines. There is much evidence that a supposed danger of atheism was a preoccupation of all literate classes at this time. *See* John Redwood, *Reason, Ridicule, and Religion: The Age of Enlightenment in England, 1660–1750* (London: Thames and Hudson, 1976).

Up to now it has been the King's good fortune that most of these people like the monarchy; but when they consider the need that the King has of them, and that if this Parliament were dissolved any other that might be assembled would be all Presbyterian, and that its first action would be to abolish the episcopacy, they become more insolent every day, and demand of the King such things that if he conceded them it would gradually upset the equilibrium, itself injurious enough, of sovereign authority so as to tip the balance towards Parliament. On the other hand, his perpetual need of money forces him to dance unhappily to the tune of the whims of that restless rabble, so that it is difficult to go forward without one party or the other being injured, unless some new way opens out that by sheer necessity may bring things into a juster proportion.

The Presbyterians are so confident of their own strength that they do not despair, given a little time, of getting even the present Parliament to abolish the bishops. I think that their hope is based on the consideration that their party is daily becoming larger, and that when it reaches a formidable size none of the parliamentarians will object to abandoning a religion in which, even at present, they do not believe. Thus the King would find himself with another Parliament even though keeping the present one, and it cannot be denied that he is exposed to this risk, and that the baselessness of the Protestant religion may give some foundation to the hopes of the Presbyterians. As their party increases, there is no doubt that the best brains of the kingdom will join it, because in England the leading minds are not strongly attached to religions, and where this check does not operate, everyone naturally likes to join the party that seems to be rising in hope of credit and authority.

At present, as the suppression of the episcopate cannot be demanded because between them the King and the Parliament would demand the suppression of the religion that they profess and solemnly swear to, the Act of Comprehension is brought forward instead, which means not only liberty of conscience but the free activity of every other sect, if indeed only the Catholic religion (as is likely) would still be excluded.[6] There is no doubt that at the first intimation that it had of the King's intention, which was to bring up this business the very day of his arrival, the Parliament met early and passed an Act directly contrary to this design, so that

---

[6] This must refer to legislation similar to the Declaration of Indulgence unsuccessfully put forward in 1663.

the King quite well understood the inclination of men's minds and did not dare to try it.

Nevertheless the Presbyterians did not even then despair of being able to bring off the coup, well knowing that not religious zeal, but the money, severity, and practices of the bishops inflame the breasts of those people with such fervour. Some of these were even Presbyterians corrupted by their gifts. These, however, will no longer have so much force when the King, persuaded of his real interest, is able to find the true opportunity to obtain this Act of Parliament, for it is certain that against the attraction of some money that they might get from the ecclesiastics will prevail the consideration of the much greater advantages that they will be able to hope for in the free exercise of a religion which, being quite independent of the King, can propagate without fear of punishment the principles most suitable for the establishment of their design.

What may happen to the King when this Act of Comprehension is passed is very difficult to judge, first because it is far off and it is impossible to predict in what circumstances it may occur, and second, because after affairs have gone along in such chaotic confusion all sorts of things may happen in a moment to give advantage or disadvantage to one party or the other, against all right, or anticipated reason.

It is certain that from such an Act the King would from the first gain greatly by the immense riches he would receive, and if he seized the occasion of a war desired by the kingdom, after having got from Parliament large votes of money to wage it, so that he would be well armed at sea, and if he should at the same time consent to the abolition of the bishops, annexing and at once selling all the property of the churches, and then after all this bringing about an immediate peace against every expectation of his subjects, it is very probable that he would find himself in a condition utterly different from the present one. This is because, the nobles dispersed and impoverished by Henry VII, the Catholic religion driven out under Queen Elizabeth, the Episcopalian religion discredited and mocked by great and small, the kingdom overturned and in confusion with the liberty of forming whatever new religions anyone thinks best, there would remain no other force for the monarchy than that of money, which would put the King into a position of being able to act without Parliament, whereas at present he has to beg in an undignified way the means of sustaining the wars that he undertakes, even for the advantage of his own subjects. They, not less fearful of their own prince than of external enemies, arm him only as well as they have to, and would rather fear something from abroad than nothing, with the sole disadvantage that they would have to fear something within.[7]

Thus at present the principles of the King of England are not to be generous, not to be benign, nor wise, nor just, but to be rich, and to be so with the reputation of a soldier and a fine man; the first in order to make himself safe by force, and the second so as to profit by the vain and proud character of the people, who cannot despise nor dislike a prince whom they think of as a great captain.

Another thing might improve the situation of the King, because this is something that weakened him when he lost it. This is the Catholic religion. There is no doubt that without the advice of the Chancellor it could have been put back, when the King returned, into such a condition (allowing the liberty of practising it, as the King desired) that now this remedy, which is still in the bud, might begin to look like ripening. But the Chancellor,[8] drawn by the interest that he found entirely in the re-establishment of the bishops, fearful of leading the kingdom back into obedience to Rome in this way, and on the other hand attracted by a certain glory in having in the kingdom rather a model than a copy of religion, diverted the mind of the King from the execution of his good ideas. This was easy for him to do by suggesting to the King a panic terror of new revolts, and of new and more incurable uncertainties.

It was not because of any such fear that the Chancellor, finding out that this shadow of Anglican religion, instead of taking on a body, was continually fading away, opportunely began to turn against it, favouring the Presbyterians[9] so as not to see a formidable party growing behind him, without having the merit of contributing anything, from his side, to its growth. He still acted in this way, without in the least prejudicing the ordinary rewards that he was getting from the protection that he provided

---

[7] This scenario of Magalotti's would not have occurred to him if he had been better acquainted with the people outside the court.

[8] Edward Hyde, first Earl of Clarendon (1609–1674). He was dismissed from the chancellorship in 1667.

[9] This erroneous statement was also made by the Venetian ambassador Pietro Mocenigo in his *relazione* to the Senate of Venice on his return in 1670. See Nicolò Barozzi and Guglielmo Berchet, eds., *Relazioni . . . lette al senato dagli ambasciatori veneti nel secolo decimosettimo,* Ser. IV—Inghilterra, vol. unico (Venezia, 1863), p. 455.

to the bishops. Indeed, the more he favoured the other party, the greater the advantages he obtained from the bishops because their avarice decreased as much as their fear increased, and he knew so well how to manage things in the discrepancy between these two commitments, that except for the lightning of the King's wrath he would still remain in authority, sustained equally by one party and the other.

But turning to what is to be hoped for the Catholic religion, opinions differ. The Catholics believe that the impossibility of ever seeing this intemperate government take any good course must finally bring men's minds to the necessity of reconciling themselves with a religion that is not incompatible either with the monarchy or with Parliament, and they assert that this cannot be other than Catholicism. I have no doubt whatever that what they say is true, but I believe that as men do not receive their disillusionments from what others tell them, but get them from their own experience, it will require such a long time to undeceive the English, that before this there may be such changes, disturbing once more the balance of these two incompatible authorities, Parliament and King, that they may no longer be any necessity of going to look for the religion that could best serve to unite them, as that one may suffice, that is the best and most suitable to the interests of the party that remains on top.

The Catholics say that their number increases daily, and that the Act of Comprehension would be the truest means of establishing religion in the kingdom. The Presbyterians promise themselves the same advantage for theirs. To say which are deceived would need information that I do not possess, the more so because I cannot use as typical the kinds of people whom I have consulted, recognizing some as too credulous Catholics, and others as Presbyterians too passionate and perverse. I do think I can say that the nobility would be Catholic and the rich men Presbyterians. The latter are without doubt much more numerous than the former, but that does not mean that they may not remain the losers, when to the former may be added the greater part of the common people, who in such a case have to be considered as a herd of cattle up before two buyers, of which there is no doubt that the Presbyterians, offering the bait of self-interest and spreading the fear of tyranny of the Pope and the King, would have some advantage, if it were not, by good fortune, that the character of the nation (for we see that liberty of belief, rather than releasing it to atheism, ties it more and more into knots of new religions) appears to allow it to be carried willingly into superstition. Thus we have a greater aversion to the bareness of the Presbyterian churches than to the nuptial ornaments with which the Catholic ones are adorned, in more perfect imitation of that New Jerusalem, seen descending from Heaven in the apparel of the Bride of Christ.

It seems a great matter that in this disturbed situation of religion and state there should be no remedy profitable to the King's own concerns; but the reason for this is very soon clear, if we consider the King surrounded by his fiercest enemies, reconciled to him not by love or by repentance, but by self-interest or ambition. And this was the policy of the Chancellor in the restoration of the King, to recapture with apppointments and honours the more restless and troublesome spirits and the most popular persons, in short the most ambitious and grasping men, and to neglect those who had risked their lives and property in the service of the King, on the supposition that such men, since they had felt themselves honoured in the days of affliction, would do the same in the days of glory,[10] and since they had had so much zeal up to that time, would have as much prudence in sympathizing with the King, if by the force of circumstances he had to leave his good and faithful subjects behind. So he might insure himself with the rewards owed them against those enemies whom the sword could not destroy, meanwhile leaving himself in peace in the expectation of better times in which it might be permissible for him to repay them handsomely for the delay in their rewards. This ill-conceived policy was dependent not so much on the faith and discretion of those people as on their powerlessness, which, as it originated mainly in their having served the King well, instead of earning them remuneration, drew contempt on them, and gave the King confidence of being able to take advantage of them without risk, in mockery of their merits and their hopes.

The result is that although such people faithfully suffer the harm of such a damaging confrontation, the King should not therefore reckon on their fidelity as before, were things to change. So poor is his condition, that without ever believing that he could also capture the hearts of his enemies, as he has their persons, he can neither free himself from their hands, nor repay his friends. For so great is the number of those who so closely besiege him, that he

---

[10] Pepys records two instances of such complaints in his *Diary*: March 7, 1661/2, and December 15, 1665. See also O. Airy's footnote in Burnet's *History of My Own Time*, 1, 177.

cannot even refill the places made vacant by natural death, according to his own ideas or rather with justice, while he constantly has to dispose of them according to the impertinent pleas of those who remain. So much so that unless they all agree to die at the same time it does not appear that the King will for a long time be able to rid himself of this sort of people, or of those who have gone to their school and soaked up their principles, and who are united by the same interests, attached to the same parties, fortified by the same abilities, and finally persuaded of the same truth, that the King neither should nor can trust them. For the fundamental reason that they remain near him is, and cannot be anything else, but to keep him without friends whose support he can rely on, to meddle in Parliament, to excite discord and feed uncertainty, to keep themselves necessary by keeping the King in a continual anxiety about their conduct.

This is what little I have been able to find out in general about the present constitution of England, and even if this is but little for making others understand it, nevertheless it may serve for the formation of a sure judgment of what the most intimate qualities of the personages whom I am going to describe may mean in this theatre of action as time goes on.

The King of England[11]

The King of England would be ugly if he were a private gentleman, but because he is the King he manages to pass as a well-made man. Nevertheless he has a very fine figure, and is free and attractive in his person and in all his motions. His complexion is swarthy, tending towards black; his hair is black, his sideburns and eyebrows very black. His eyes are bright and shining, but set strangely in his face, his nose large and bony, but still well made. His mouth is wide, with thin lips, and he has a short chin. His cheeks are marked across under the eyes with two deep and prominent lines or wrinkles that begin near the middle of the nose and go towards the corners of the eyes, getting thinner and thinner and vanishing before they get there. He wears a wig, almost entirely black, and very thick and curly above his forehead, which makes him look sadder but without giving him any trace of grimness; on the contrary his appearance is sad but not grim.

---

[11] This is an excellent example of Magalotti's talent for "lightning sketches."

Indeed a certain smiling look coming from the width of his mouth so greatly clears and softens the roughness of his features that he pleases rather than terrifies.

He is very light-hearted about religion, but if he were obliged to reflect upon it I do not think he would find salvation outside the Catholic faith. He has a great and able mind, and with this a maturity of judgment and a marvellous clarity of intelligence. Nobody understands affairs better than he, and nobody manages politics with greater mastery.[12] His affability, goodness, clemency, and gentleness are without equal, and he respects the laws of friendship. He is thoroughly conversant with the temperament of his subjects, and in a short time he can discover the weak point of anyone, and find the way to exploit it.

On the other hand his fiercest enemies are diligence and business. He worships comforts, pleasures, and practical jokes, hates implacably all sorts of work, and loves with the greatest enthusiasm every kind of play and diversion. Serious men terrify him, merry and amusing ones fill him with delight. He is generous because he does not want the trouble of saying no; besides, he can hate without harming and like without helping. Therefore the number of his friends increases enormously, for they cost little, and those who are more impudent in their demands are more fortunate in getting them.

Only love makes him liberal by choice, and in this case he is generous beyond measure. His inclinations are towards sensuousness rather than bestiality, and he enjoys spiritual, rather than bodily relations. It is not that the latter have not demanded their rôle, but now and for some time past it seems that his delight in sensuality is less than that in drinking in the company of friends, without always observing an exact measure of sobriety.

They say that his courtesy and affability are not so entirely the effect of royal magnanimity that some little part of them may not be due to the habit formed in his youth of adopting the humble manners of a poor and private nobleman. It perhaps also results from this, that in the beginning of his inclination he lets himself be so transported by impetuosity that in the courtesies of a lover he forgets the decorum of a king.

Of bodily exercises he most dislikes hunting, and most enjoys tennis. He plumes himself on a great knowledge of fortifica-

---

[12] The political acuteness of Charles II is recognized even by Whig historians. Magalotti seems to have sensed it at once.

tions, and to facilitate their use he claims to have found new rules that he has had engraved in two outline figures on the faces of a medal.[13]

To hear him talk, he seems to take great delight in every noble curiosity, not excluding the new experiments and natural science; but even if he manages to have some taste for these things, he is not capable of having any esteem for them, nor for those who practise them.[14]

The Queen

The Queen[15] (as I was told by a friend of whom I inquired before seeing her) is beautiful, because never in this world do you hear that a queen is ugly. Nevertheless considering her as if she were a private lady, one might have some reservations about this. First of all, her stature is small for a woman and a shade tall for a dwarf. The lower half of her face is very narrow, so that she has a pointed chin; her mouth is large and her teeth are appalling. Unfortunately she is always showing them because she never stops smiling, and she accompanies her smile with certain twistings of the head and by thrusting her face forward. She would not prejudice her decorum if she abstained from this. Her nose is a little small, but well shaped and very round, her eyes are angelic in their size and in the splendour of their very dark pupils. Her forehead is large and majestic and her hair is extremely abundant, dark, and shining. Her complexion is a little dark for England, but very light for Portugal, if indeed it has not had a little attention according to the custom of one country or the other. Her bearing is

---

[13] Miss Crinò has discovered in the British Museum two different medals (*Medallic Illustrations*, plate LVI, 10, and plate LVII, 1) coined in 1673. In the book *Medallic Illustrations of the History of Great Britain and Ireland to the Death of George II,* 2 vols. (London, British Museum, 1885; reprinted 1969), I, p. 558, these designs are identified as being by Sir Jonas Moore, the King's Master of Ordnance.

[14] Magalotti was probably right; but he certainly was influenced by something that he had been told in the Low Countries, namely that Charles habitually referred to the Fellows of the Royal Society as "my fools." See W. E. K. Middleton, *Royal Society Notes and Records,* 31 (1977), 13−16. On the other hand Samuel de Sorbière professed to be surprised by the extent of the King's knowledge of these matters (*Relation d'un voyage en Angleterre* [Paris, 1664], p. 79). But he was scarcely a competent judge.

[15] Catherine, daughter of the Duke of Braganza who became King John IV of Portugal. She was married to Charles on May 21, 1662.

correct, her dress ordinary and more like that of a widow than of a young princess.

From the beginning her education was watched over by a very careful mother and then, according to the custom of Portugal, which also applies to royal daughters, she was sent among the nuns to a convent. The dying wish of her father, King John, was that when she came to marriageable age she should be given to the young Duke of Aveiro. The Queen, her mother, out of revenge for an old enmity to the mother of the Duke, would not have it; the Duke, offended at this, as soon as he heard of the first negotiations for a treaty with England, thinking to spoil them completely, gave the Chancellor to understand that the Princess, because of her slender figure, the dry temper of her constitution, and the extraordinary frequency and abundance of her menses, was firmly judged incapable of bearing children.[16]

These reports, which unfortunately are seen to be true, found the Chancellor entirely disposed to the conclusion of the Portuguese marriage, urged to it up to that time by the sole motive of destroying the one with Parma,[17] not so much to escape a Spanish alliance as to disappoint the negotiations of the Earl of Bristol, whom he sought to ruin, not less by discrediting him than by every other means. Now by these reports from the Duke there was added to these two motives—his pro-French policy and his quarrel with Bristol—a third very efficacious one. This was the interest of his daughter,[18] who had already become the wife of the Duke of York, and this was because the hoped-for sterility of the Queen assured the crown to his line. He did not delay the conclusion of the marriage in any way, and it was effected with the dowry of the two fortresses of Tangiers and Bombay and [two million][19] cruzados, half on the arrival of the bride and half a year later, although this last instalment has not yet been paid.[20] On the part of England there was promised continued assistance to Portugal in order to

---

[16] On May 7, 1668, Charles wrote to his sister telling her that his wife had just had a miscarriage. See C. M. Hartmann, *The King My Brother* (London, 1954), p. 216.

[17] It was proposed that Charles should marry Maria Caterina Farnese, the daughter of the Duke of Parma.

[18] Anne Hyde (1637–1671), who married the Duke of York in 1660. Her two daughters Mary and Anne both became Queens of England. This accusation against the Chancellor, current at the time, is most probably untrue.

[19] A lacuna in the manuscript. See e.g. David Ogg, *England in the Reign of Charles II* (London, 1956), p. 187.

[20] It was paid in 1670.

obtain for her a secure and honourable peace,[21] either by force of arms or by negotiation.

She has an ordinary mind, inclined to piety, or rather superstition: masses, rosaries, vespers, sermons, and complines take up all her attention. Outside of this her chief employment is to be with her ladies morning and evening, and there, on a chair, rule over the chatter of the women for three or four hours a day, leaving this at times to play at ombre in the same room, calling to the game both ladies and noblemen indiscriminately. The rest of the day goes by in saying Hail Mary's or in chattering with her women, for she takes no delight in reading or music or painting, or in any other thing imaginable. Among the men and women of her court she has nobody able to guide her, for she never gains the confidence or affection of anyone. She becomes irritated quite without reason, and once she has come to dislike a servant, nothing can be done about it. She has the highest opinion of herself, her family, and her country, which makes her inflexible in her decisions, for in addition to the ordinary gift of obstinacy that she has as a Portuguese she has that which comes from being a woman and a queen. It is perilous with her to begin a comparison between the affairs and customs of Portugal and those of other countries, because unless you lower the latter below the ground and raise the former above the heavens, you will not say enough to please her, indeed you will do more than enough to offend her. This idea is not at all self-deception, but an affectation due to ambition, which will not let her seem to have left less in her brother's[22] house than she found in that of her husband.

By nature she is very susceptible to pleasures, but whether through virtue or ineptitude, not only does she content herself with those she has with the King, but is as temperate as she can be in these, since, finding that too continuous an indulgence, whether from a superabundance of blood or from excessive pleasure, causes extraordinary and ill-timed purges, she fears that she may too soon bring herself to the point of despairing of having children. In spite of all that, she is not careful about eating food full of very hot condiments, thinking to put things right well enough by abstaining from wine, and in fact she drinks only once at the end of the meal, taking a very large draught of water at that

---

[21] The treaty of Lisbon, February 13, 1668, ensured the independence of Portugal from Spain.

[22] The ill-fated King Alphonso VI (1643–1675).

time. She is subject to burning fevers of great severity, from one of which she nearly died. That was what moved the Chancellor to induce the Duke of Richmond[23] to marry [Frances] Stuart[24] against the wishes of the King, recognizing in her beauty a lasting nourishment for the fervid desires of the King, and in the nobility of her blood (for she was of royal descent) a splendour enough for her to be queen. The Chancellor wished to be certain that if the Queen died the King would not know at once where to turn to have a clear succession but would have to look for a queen outside the kingdom, with the loss of all the time that always goes with arranging royal marriages. The Chancellor would add to this every delay that he promised himself to procure in favour of the children of the Duke [of York], interposing obstacles to the arrangement of every match. And this was his greatest mistake because the King, touched where he was most sensitive, began to give ear to reports about the Chancellor to which he would not listen before, and induced in this way to recognize their existence, found them to be true.

For her household list the Queen has sixty thousand pounds sterling from the King, of which he keeps back twenty thousand, and takes upon himself the provisions for her, her ladies, and all those who should have them in her court, also the stable, the liveries, the pay of the lower servants, and a part of the provisions of the noble attendants that a heretic queen would keep. This is because of the additional expenses that she has, being a Catholic. I have said that the King pays a part of these provisions, and this part consists of the emoluments that these offices used to have, according to the ancient fees of the royal house, when money was scarcer in England and in consequence was worth more. But now that these provisions have increased, all the surplus remains at the expense of the Queen. After this, the greatest burden that remains for her is the maintenance of her church (besides the private chapel at Whitehall) in St. James's Palace, to which she goes across the park on every feast day. This includes the community of Por-

---

[23] Charles Stuart, third Duke of Richmond (1639–1672). It seems unlikely that the Chancellor would have needed to induce the Duke to marry Frances Stuart, for he was madly in love with her, and eloped with her in defiance of the King, in March, 1667. Even though the marriage suited the Chancellor's plans, it probably contributed greatly to his disgrace, for Charles, also in love with Frances Stuart, believed that Clarendon had promoted it.

[24] Frances Teresa Stuart (1647–1702), maid-of-honour to the Queen, and a celebrated beauty.

tuguese Franciscans, set up entirely by her, which contains eleven priests, including the Dominicans and the Benedictines, who are equal in number (and she gives each one about two suits of civilian clothes a year), as well as the provisions for the Grand Almoner, four ordinary almoners, and seven or eight others between chaplains and clerics. It all comes to eight thousand pounds sterling. There are also the gifts made to the maids-of-honour, and special ones when they are married, although in this matter there are no rules other than her own tastes and generosity.

On this subject I should mention that the custom of giving these presents to the maids-of-honour, usually as much by the King as by the Queen, was brought in to augment the smallness of the allowances that they have from the royal house, which consist of room and board and ten pounds a year. They have to find their own clothes. But in this court none of them is so stupid that they cannot get maintenance and extras; and the governesses, whose pay is forty pounds a year, are tactful enough to let them enjoy the fruits of their industry.

Before leaving this subject I will say that the Court of England maids-of-honour and ladies-in-waiting are not the same (even aside from the first lady-in-waiting), since the maids-of-honour have to be girls or at least unmarried, and not only may they not enter the Queen's bedroom, but strictly (this was the practice at one time, although, the King having given one or another permission to do so, the thing has been taken advantage of) they ought not even to enter the dressing room, but stay in the presence chamber, or as we should say, *sala del baldacchino*. The ladies-in-waiting enter the bedroom, and these are among the greatest ladies of the court and of the realm. They obtain nothing from this title besides the dignity.

Turning now to the Queen's household list, it would seem that she would have to have a very great deal of money saved up, for she does not enjoy spending anything at all about her person. In spite of this she never has a hundred pounds in her cabinet, giving everything to everyone who asks, provided that they are Portuguese, so that there is no one great or small, priest or friar, silly woman, sailor, or boatman of that nation who lives otherwise than at the expense of the Queen. One great drain for her purse is Don Francesco di Melo and his sister. The latter came to London to be her first lady-in-waiting although, surprised by a weakness of the eyes that very quickly increased to complete blindness, she did not even enter into possession of the appointment, but retired to a private house where she remains, occupied with acts of piety, without ever receiving anyone and, excused because of her infirmity, comes only very rarely to visit the Queen.[25] Her brother, who is now ambassador at The Hague, will come back to London in the same rôle, when he has finished his embassy there. Since he left Lisbon he has lived and still lives, as one might say, supported by the Queen, who is charmed by the vanity of having a Portuguese ambassador at the Court of England. The Count of Castel Melhor[26], although he is a cousin to don Francesco, has never been willing to be responsible for this, but the Queen with her usual obstinacy put herself out to maintain the latter at her own expense and was allowed to do so.

As for her English servants, they can hope for nothing more when they have drawn their pay; and as for any protection from her in case of need, no one, English or Portuguese, expects it, so far is she from interfering, or becoming heated on anyone's account. This is because of the shadow cast on her spirit by her fear of the Chancellor, which leaves her without the courage to undertake anything. In spite of this, if she wished to, she would be able to get the King to do many things, not by any great influence that she may have, but by the inability that the King has to shake off the yoke when anyone has the temerity to put it on, and to let a matter alone, even completely, when he finds that someone else will set himself to look after it for him. It should be added that he loves her for her goodness, and although she does not succeed in being admired, she would do so as soon as she began to torment him with tiresome persistence and to ask for things. At first there was mutual coldness, because when she began to pout she soon became aware that in matters of love the King changed his nature, not allowing either practical jokes or moodiness. But now she has become used to bearing her cross in peace, admitting to her presence, with self possession and goodwill, the Countess of Castlemaine[27] even with her little children.

---

[25] Don Francesco de Melo, later the Portuguese ambassador to the English court, died in London in 1678. His sister died there in 1670 (Crinò).

[26] Don Luiz de Sousa y Vasconcellos, Count of Castello Melhor, the chief minister and almost the ruler of Portugal for several years. He was deposed by a palace revolution and forced to flee to France at about the time that Magalotti was in London.

[27] Charles's mistress *en titre*.

The Duke of York

The features of the Duke of York are more oddly assorted than those of the King, so that he appears to have a certain fierceness that substitutes the idea of a severe prince for the air of a fine gentleman, which he lacks. His stature, although noticeably less than that of the King, is nevertheless average. His complexion may be called light in colour. Besides, all the outlines of his face are prominent: a square forehead, the eyes large, swollen, and deep blue, the nose curved and rather large, the lips pale and thick, and the chin rather pointed. He wears a wig between light and dark, and has a blond beard and eyebrows. Only his bearing does not fit, as it is in no way in accord with that character of severe majesty which does duty for good looks; he walks hurriedly, bent and without dignity, and his way of dressing, always careless and matter-of-fact, goes with the small attention he gives to all his movements.

Whether he may be religious or not, his soul does not gain or lose tranquillity, for he flatters himself with the belief that if religion is necessary to salvation, any religion will do. His reputation for bravery has harmed him much more than the death of his father, his poverty, and his exile; since, esteemed for his actions in the Flemish wars, where he commanded a regiment in the service of Spain, he succeeded in getting the English people to want him to be king instead of his brother. Even in the time of Cromwell there were intrigues on foot, managed by a Jesuit, to have him marry Cromwell's daughter and to settle the crown on him, supposing that the favour of making him king unjustly might prevail over their offence of having slaughtered his father and iniquituously oppressed his brother.[28] These motives for the love and esteem procured for him by the opinion of his courage— which, as I have said elsewhere, is the most appropriate bait to entice the people of England into subjection to their princes— awoke such jealousy in the mind of the King on his return that, to make the Duke just as odious and abhorred, he promoted his marriage to the daughter of the Chancellor, then maid-of-honour to the Princess of Orange,[29] suggesting that to marry her would add to his glory by giving her what he had promised in the transports of his ardent lust, when he had enjoyed her favours.

---

[28] The initially greater popularity of the Duke is supported by Burnet (*History*, 1, 295), but we may have doubts about this supposed intrigue.

[29] This was Charles' sister, Mary (1631–1660), the Princess Royal, who married the Prince of Orange.

All the difficulties in this affair, which gleams of reason disclosed to the youthful mind of the Duke, were overcome by the arts of the Chancellor and the indifference of the Duke's most trusted servants. However, the thing was done, and perhaps the King repented of it, foreseeing that the sterility of the Queen is not sufficiently compensated by the fecundity of the Duchess (considering that she comes from a lower class) to hold down the unquiet spirits of the kingdom, many of whom would be pacified and abandon their present unease, making a bed for sedition, when they saw as guarantor of the royal line a prince born of the royal blood with no admixture from the lower classes. It is certain that if the King dies without children, as he is at present, then even though the crown should pass quietly on to the head of the Duke without disturbing the public tranquillity, having to leave it to the children that he has had from the Duchess would cost him at least some preoccupation which would perhaps not happen if he had had them from another woman who was not of a lower class.

The Duke is impetuous and violent, and consequently inconsiderate and unreasonable most of the time. He has not much penetration into political affairs, because his rough and impatient spirit does not let him stop for long to examine things, but makes him follow his first impulses blindly. Nevertheless he is very often influenced by people, and once he has chosen them it is not so easy for him to free himself from their sway; his mind is always like wax, ready to receive and retain indelibly every slight impression of their ideas, without considering whether these proceed from reason, or from self-interest, or malignity, or ambition. To everyone except those people he is inflexible, no matter if they come armed not only with reason, but with evidence itself. He lives on good terms with the King, not entirely because he has to and not entirely because he wants to. He loves his wife but does not worship her as he once did; and she, who knows his weakness, has put a bridle on him that he scarcely manages to throw off entirely, though it is loosened sometimes. His lack of application would be equal to that of the King, if on the contrary the much greater obligation that the King has did not make his appear incomparably greater. In his inclination towards sensuality he is the opposite of the King, since he cares little for the more innocent preparations for tenderness, and longs for the occasion for the release of a vicious brutality. He is extraordinarily proud of his knowledge of his profession, in the exercise of which he acutely feels the spur of glory, which he cannot be induced to share with anyone at all. He is a very good shot, especially at birds on the wing and almost always when on horseback. He is affable and courteous with foreigners, speaks several languages, but none well, and in conversation he has little ability to express himself, or to use gestures, and in no way has he the style and character of a prince.

At present he seems tranquil, after great excitement provoked in him by his wife in connection with what happened to his father-in-law. Perhaps it will not be long before Coventry[30] returns to him in the old peace and confidence, although the omnipotence of that lady[31] and his open way of co-operating in the ruin of the Chancellor threw him down from the place that he held in the Duke's favour. When this happens it will be an effect of the Duke's incapacity to free himself from someone to whom he has once been devoted.

The Duchess of York

The Duchess[32] is the most frank and sincere woman in the world, because she shows her thoughts clearly in her face. Not to waste much time on her portrait, it will be enough, to see her portrayed to the life, to show what must be on the outside of a woman who internally has neither religion nor faith; a woman obstinate, proud, vindictive, hot-tempered, deceitful, cruel, scornful, and worshipping gluttony and amusements. In these few words are included all the reports that pass for the truth openly professed by the voices of all and confirmed by the universal hatred and abhorrence of all her closest servants (to whom she is insupportable because of her scorn, her ingratitude, and her arrogance), the court, the household, and all the three kingdoms. However, it could well be believed that such a nature could not exist without the help of a great spirit, which sparkles out through her eyes with

---

[30] This was Sir William Coventry (ca. 1627–1686), fourth son of Thomas, Lord Coventry. He became private secretary to the Duke of York in 1660, and in 1662 one of the commissioners of the navy; for this reason there are many references to him in Pepys's *Diary*. He was a very able parliamentarian, and his speeches in the Commons contributed to the fall of Clarendon in 1667.

[31] This powerful lady was the Countess of Castlemaine. Clarendon had from the first been disturbed by her influence on the King, and she knew this, and did everything possible to obtain the dismissal of the Chancellor.

[32] Magalotti's judgment of Anne Hyde, Duchess of York, is harsh indeed, although her gluttony was well known, and Burnet and Pepys agree on her haughtiness, but she seems to have been no less religious than most of her contemporaries, and indeed became a Catholic before her death.

a flash of lightning that frightens instead of comforting. They say that she has been very beautiful, and this is indeed likely, in view of the ill-considered decision of the Duke to marry her. But now the superfluous fat that she keeps putting on day by day has so altered the proportions of a very fine figure and a most lovely face, that it is very hard to recognize them in her tallness, in the delicacy of her complexion (because her cheeks are a little roughened by some pock-marks) and her bosom, and in the splendour of her chestnut hair.

This much can be said about this woman, as we do not wish to outrage the truth unworthily by following too rigorously the ordinary characterizations, made up in order to present to the public with respect the vices and defects of the great.

Prince Rupert

Prince Rupert,[33] younger son of the Elector of Heidelberg, has from his earliest years followed the fortunes of the royal house of England, to which he came to seek his own, up to the time of the death of the King. In the civil wars he held some command until, a few parliamentary vessels having rebelled, he was made Admiral of these. Going with them to the West Indies in order to see to securing some of the forts there for the present King, who was then in France, he was overtaken by a hurricane near one of the Antilles, but saved himself with a page and a man-servant in a boat, seeing the vessel perish before his eyes. After returning to Europe and disembarking at Marseilles, he became one of the King's followers, profiting by every chance he had during the exile of the royal family to master the profession of arms. Since the King's return he has several times commanded at sea, and on every occasion he has shown a prodigious courage, which would be still more admirable if it were entirely the effect of conscious obedience to the choice of an intrepid mind, and if it did not consist very greatly (as many believe) of thoughtlessness and temerity.

From this we see that in battle the actions of his head are not to be considered nearly as much as those of his heart, although he is

---

[33] Prince Rupert (1619–1682), the third son of Elizabeth, sister of Charles I, was thus the cousin of Charles II. Magalotti seems to have been very greatly impressed with the Prince's virtues; in a letter to Viviani from London dated February 29, 1667/8 (Biblioteca Riccardiana, Florence, MS 2487, fol. 92r) he expatiates on his luck in being in London when Prince Rupert arrived from Portugal, and does not even mention a very interesting meeting of the Royal Society that he had attended two days earlier.

indefatigable in every operation and the rank of captain does not serve to exempt him from every least obligation of the private soldier or the sailor, even if there is no need for him to assume them. And really his skill in the arts of the sailor and the engineer is incredible. He manages to perfect with his own hands—which are always scratched and calloused by the continual use of the file, chisel, and adze—whatever mechanical device it comes into his head to make. He delights in odours[34] and in chemistry and has a very good knowledge of a great deal of natural history. He is affable, courteous, and obliging, without any abuse of his princely dignity in his use of manners more appropriate to a courteous nobleman.

He goes to Parliament as Duke of Cumberland and Knight of the Garter, and goes into the Privy Council but without taking part in the most sensitive affairs; he has quarters in the palace and draws from the King a pension of four thousand miserable pounds sterling a year. There are those who praise him to the skies for very great judgment in political matters, but of those whom I have chanced to ask, I have found that a minority are of this opinion.

In the last battle, after the victory, he had the misfortune to slip while on board, fell and was wounded by hitting his head on a nail. He had to be trepanned and had a hard time recovering. It seems that he has now got over it; I think, however, that the wound remains unhealed, and that he always wears some protection concealed by his wig.

The prince is perhaps fifty-one years old[35] (but I may be mistaken in this), tall in stature, slight and slender of figure, has a noble appearance but is not handsome, his face being long, gaunt, dark, and disfigured by the small-pox. His eyes are light and deep; he has an aquiline nose, a large mouth, and thin lips. At present his clothes are practical and as negligent as they can be, and his table by far inferior to those of many of the chief noblemen of London. His quality makes him embarrassed at nothing, and he goes with everyone and everywhere, even as far as eating in the ordinary public taverns, paying his bill like everyone else, as is the custom in England, even of the greatest nobles. This liberty of his arises partly from his off-hand manner, in part also, it may be,

---

[34] This word (*odori*) is interesting because of Magalotti's much later and very extensive writings about perfumes.

[35] He was born on December 16, 1619, so that he was forty-eight at the time of Magalotti's visit.

from a desire to spend less than he might. This is also seen in the moderation with which he rules himself even in the fervour of his desires, which (at least recently) cost him little trouble and little money.

As to religion, although he is a Calvinist, he does not fail to go with the King to the prayers of the Protestants, for on this subject his character is easy and accommodating.

The Queen Mother

At present the Queen Mother[36] contents herself with the impression that she made and the authority that she has had in England in times past. Rewarded by the power that she exercised over the character of her husband, but realizing from his unhappy end that her principles are not the right ones for guiding the kings of England, she resigns herself to her present retirement from all business. She says she is content with those acts of reverent esteem that she receives personally from the King in his palace when she is in London, and with the eighty thousand pounds a year that are generously paid to her wherever she may be, half from the profits from her dowry and half from the pension left her by the dead King.

For some time now she has lived almost entirely in France, given so much to things of the spirit that she is becoming, especially to her ladies-in-waiting and maids-of-honour, an inquisitive and intolerable investigator of every little weakness of everyone at her court.

The Duke of Monmouth

James, Duke of Monmouth,[37] natural son of the King, was born in France to an Englishwoman who had dedicated herself to the pleasures of both the nations. She had sexual relations with the King during the time of his troubles, discovered that she was

---

[36] Henrietta Maria (1609–1669), Queen Consort of Charles I. She had finally left England in 1665. Her political activities had proved disastrous to her husband and herself.

[37] James, Duke of Monmouth (1649–1685) was a natural son of Charles II by Lucy Walters. I do not know of any authority for "La Soccarière." According to to Wood, vol. 1, col. 888, the child was placed in the care of Stephen Gough or Goffe, D.D., a chaplain to the Queen-Mother. The "Scottish girl" was Anne Scott, Countess of Buccleuch in her own right, whose income was nearer £10,000 than £6,000.

pregnant, and claimed that the child was his. He was therefore given to a bastard of the Duke of Bellegarde called La Soccarière (although known everywhere as M. de Montbrun) to be brought up, and stayed with him until the King, his father, was recalled to his kingdom. Then the King called him to his court, creating him Duke and Knight of the Garter, and when he was fourteen years old made him marry a Scottish girl, herself very young, pretty rather than beautiful, an heiress with an income of six thousand pounds, administered independently, however, by the mother-in-law, because the Duke, to put it briefly, would be reduced to nothing; he has nothing certain of his own but a thousand pounds a year from his office of gentleman of the bedchamber.

He has a very fine figure and a most handsome face, on which scarcely appear the first signs of a beard; but he is rather weak and ignorant, and as cold as can be. He is most unhappy in conversation and in paying compliments, with all his French schooling, his experience at court, and his acquaintance with so many princes. His inclination leads him to the pleasures of the senses and of wine; he has lately recovered somewhat from the latter, but in the former he is easily pleased, and very often has paid, in the hands of the doctors, the penalty of his too ignoble and imprudent sensuality. Now he has just returned from a voyage in France, where he gave more satisfaction to the eyes of the ladies than to any other of their senses, for in him there is more of ostentation than utility, in regard to the chief needs of that sex. There will be a place later to discuss the reason for his journey.

The King dotes on him and is beside himself at not being able to get a man with any style out of such fine young material. He would have liked to put in his way some good man who with his conversation might instill in him the delights of knowledge, but the nature of the Duke, which prefers the company of low, rough persons to that of men of circumstance and honour, was the reason that one to whom he was given as a trial retired politely, foreseeing that with him he would either have to become a boy, or lose his reputation, or accept being mistreated, or finally to break off relations with him. All that the King was able to obtain was a mere beginning of application, which quickly vanished, to the study of languages, of which the Duke speaks only those two that he learned by necessity. In spite of all this the King cannot in the least moderate his tender affection for him, which sometimes impels him to kiss and embrace him in public.

He has quarters in the palace, which is the only prerogative brought him by the admixture of royal blood that he has in him. Nevertheless he does not come into prominence in anything, according to the prejudicial custom practised in England with bastards of the blood royal, who get no consideration and are not acknowledged at all.[38] The King has given him a coat of arms, on which, among others, are quartered the arms of Ireland. When speaking to him the King never utters the name of duke, but always calls him by his own name.

General Monk

General George Monk,[39] Duke of Albemarle, of an English family of the county of Devonshire that has become great in the person of the present Duke, is sixty-six[40] years old. He is short and stout, and without either the courtesy of a nobleman or the demeanour of a great captain. He is a good man, and so full of courage that there is no room in him to hold any other virtues except his loyalty to the King and his sincerity with his friends. But his great experience has made him the one who understands the country better than anyone else. On the other hand his manner would not be worth as much elsewhere, for he has seen little outside England. His greatest blemish is his slowness in making up his mind, and his best quality is his rapidity in action; in fact he is always the first in this. He lives contented with his ample rewards, meddles little with affairs, loves repose. His ambition is as moderate as his character; he smokes, drinks, and listens to everyone.

Lord Arlington

Lord Arlington,[41] whose family name is Bennet, acts at present as first minister, and in truth has great power over the mind of the King. At first he was simply an assistant to the Earl of

---

[38] In view of the titles of nobility given to the King's bastards, this statement seems strange.

[39] George Monk or Monck, first Duke of Albemarle (1608–1670), second son of Sir Thomas Monck. His intense involvement in affairs for most of his life cannot be dealt with in a note (see *DNB*). At the time of Magalotti's visit he was First Lord of the Treasury, but he was not active in this office.

[40] He was fifty-nine.

[41] Henry Bennet, Lord Arlington (1618–1685) later Earl of Arlington. Magalotti is correct in his facts about him, and his estimate agrees with the contemporary opinion as far as it goes.

Bristol, under whose tutelage he gained his first knowledge of affairs. Then as secretary of the Duke he found himself handling all the negotiations with the King of France. He went on to the Court of Madrid, where he carried out his commissions with distinction, serving his prince usefully and most faithfully. He was always of the Earl of Bristol's party. When the King returned he was Keeper of the Privy Purse until, in spite of the Chancellor, he was made Secretary of State.

He is generous to his friends and very affable to deal with, although by some people he is accused (in my opinion without any reason) of being too haughty. His talents are nearer to being mediocre than to being astonishing, but still they are not so much inferior to his needs that with the addition of his fidelity the King cannot be contented with them. His greatest imperfections are in having little patience when listening to the long-winded talk of the other councillors, and his own great arrogance. For all that, he deserves to be considered the best servant that the King has around him. Some people will have it that the King has had two other motives for liking him besides those already mentioned: the first is that he put . . .;[42] the other, that he revealed many of the actions of the Duke during the time when he was his secretary. What is admirable in him is the moderation with which he uses his favour with the King himself, although he knows better than anyone else how much he could tyrannize over him, considering the King's nature, unable to defend himself from the power of all those of whom he is fond. He still behaves towards the Duke with great respect, because he considers, with careful shrewdness, the future and the things that might possibly happen then.

Joseph Williamson

I shall speak here of Joseph Williamson,[43] not because of his position but, on the contrary, because of the esteem that he enjoys

---

[42] In the Strozzi manuscript there is only a sign much like an ampersand. Miss Crinò deduces, almost certainly correctly, that this refers to the Countess of Castlemaine, citing Burnet's *History*, 1, 182: "Bennet and Berkeley had the management of the mistress."

[43] Magalotti's assessment of Joseph Williamson (1633–1701) is sound, although the *DNB* gives no authority for some of his biographical statements. Magalotti may have been told by Williamson that he was at first dismissed by Arlington, and about the help that he had from the Archbishop. Williamson had several other sources of emolument besides those mentioned by Magalotti. He followed Lord Brouncker as President of the Royal Society in 1677.

and because of his close connection with Lord Arlington, whose chief assistant he now is. He is a gentleman, one of those customarily so called in England, as I shall explain when discussing the English nobility. During his youth he lived for a time as a scholar in an Oxford college, in great poverty. Through the help of the present Archbishop of Canterbury, then Bishop of London, he obtained a post in the office of Sir [Edward] Nicholas,[44] Secretary of State before the time of Lord Arlington. As this knight was very old, the young man, being clever and diligent, came to be the Secretary's chief assistant. He had already travelled in France as the tutor of a private gentleman called Thomas Lee, and had a good command of French, as well as of some other language that he had studied out of mere curiosity. He came to have some knowledge of worldly affairs, so that he very soon came to manage the business of the secretariat by himself. Meanwhile, because of his age, Secretary Nicholas had become less and less able to perform the duties of his office. Deceived by someone who led him to believe that the King was about to confer the post on one of his children, with no other security than hope, Williamson let himself be persuaded to resign it into the hands of the King, who immediately gave it to Sir [Henry] Bennet, Keeper of the Privy Purse, who is now Lord Arlington.

The first thing that Lord Arlington did was to dismiss Williamson at once from the secretariat, considering him as the intimate favourite of his predecessor; but he very soon realized that he needed him for his knowledge of affairs and recalled him to his old position, which he still holds, retaining the closest ties of principle and of confidence. From this arises the esteem that the King and the court have for him, the courtesy and respect of the ministers of foreign princes, and finally the great emoluments that he draws from his appointments, for besides that in the secretariat, he is Keeper of the Papers of the King, or rather of the Crown. As documents often have to be produced for Parliament and for private persons, this is worth a considerable amount to him. He is also Under-Secretary of the council; and in total, with other small perquisites, he is said to have made himself a nest-egg of forty thousand pounds in ready money.

He is a tall man of very good appearance, clever, diligent, courteous, and affable. He speaks Italian, French, and Spanish

---

[44] Sir Edward Nicholas (1593–1669), retired from his office of Secretary of State in 1662.

well, and writes Latin with complete mastery. He is not presumptuous, and therefore he is very inquisitive in getting information
from anybody about things that he has not understood. People
consider him obliging and he has a way of knowing how to keep his
old friends with fidelity and respect. Many people praise him,
others complain about him; some say that he counterfeits his good
qualities and some maintain that they are rooted in the depths of
his nature. He is not well grounded outside of the things that pass
through his hands from the nature of his office, and the philosophy
and scholastic theology that he studied at Oxford are about the
only strong points of his erudition. Finally, the Court of England
has no post or position which he is not now thought competent to
fill.

The Earl of Bristol

There are two people in England who should in justice be
called great men, although neither one nor the other is making
that impression at present.

The first, who is the Earl of Bristol,[45] of the ancient Digby
family, did so at an earlier time, and the world did justice to him
with deserved applause. He is a Catholic without embarrassment,
a very good soldier and an excellent politician. In his first occupation of Secretary of State he is believed to have had few equals; Lord
Arlington and Francis Slingsby, then his assistants, attest that
while he himself was writing, he dictated two dispatches at the
same time, for France and for Ireland. He is indefatigable in
writing and never satisfied with the writing of others.

He was an enemy to the Chancellor, and the beginning of this
enmity was in France, when the King was there; it increased
greatly in Flanders and became irreconcilable over the business of
the two marriages of the King and the Duke. At one time he tried
to ruin his enemy by a rash accusation of treason, which was not
proven, of selling offices when the King returned, of using un-
worthy means to assure the marriage of his daughter to the Duke,
and finally of prejudicing the royal succession by the choice of the
Princess of Portugal. They say that on this occasion he changed his
religion; however it might have been in his mind, it is a sure thing

---

[45] George Digby, second Earl of Bristol (1612–1677). He was a man of
great ability but unstable character who was unsuccessful in most of his
undertakings. Magalotti's sketch is reasonably accurate, but Bristol was not
more licentious than many of his contemporaries.

that in England, if you want to be heard in Parliament, you must not be proved to be a recusant.

He is unfortunate in his children. The eldest, who is married, is impotent; he has been cut for the stone and is almost out of his mind. Master Digby, who is the second, is the captain of a ship and is the least unhappy. He went to Rome to fight the Earl of Sunderland, of the Spencer family, who were favourites in the times of Edward the Second. This Earl, finding himself on the point of having to marry the second daughter of the Earl of Bristol, left England hurriedly and went to Italy, although after the duel he decided to marry her, after she had been refused by the Earl of Oxford and others. There are three daughters, one married to the Baron of Moll in Flanders, but she is separated from him and although she lives in London her father does not see her. The second is the Countess of Sunderland referred to above, and the third is still unmarried.

The fall of the Chancellor gave an opportunity to his friends to call him back from his exile, during which he was wandering unknown through the kingdom under various disguises. His return has seemed to be out of the pure generosity of the King, but his strongest support has been that of Lord Arlington who, grateful to him for the origin and advancement of his fortunes, showed his thanks in this way. It is a rare thing and worthy of great admiration with what respect he speaks of him.

Finally, the strong points of the Earl of Bristol are the sword and the pen; his ornament is poetry; his weaknesses are prodigality and licentiousness.

Sir Robert Moray

The other man is not so well known beyond the seas, but he whom I have just named will perchance not disdain to be seen thus from near at hand. This is Sir Robert Moray,[46] of one of the best families of Scotland, knighted by the present King; a good soldier, doctor, and minister; generous, charitable, magnanimous, does not worry about anything, has no ambition, is indifferent to all the vicissitudes of fortune. By temperament the man is the most hot-tempered in the world, and is never seen to be angry with anybody. When he was accused by the Chancellor and others

---

[46] Sir Robert Moray or Murray (d. 1673). Magalotti's enthusiastic estimate agrees with that of his contemporaries. Moray was, however, knighted by Charles I in 1643, and not by Charles II.

among his enemies of sorcery, and of being against the King, it did him no harm at all. He is a Presbyterian, but as a good subject and counsellor of his prince, persuaded him for his own good to support the bishops. He is one of the treasurers for Scotland, whence he comes and goes, but the King likes to keep him there, for he is a man with very clean hands, in whom he trusts. He would have made him an earl, but he did not seem to care for it.

He learned the profession of arms in France, where he served first as lieutenant and later as colonel—in a Scottish regiment, if I am not mistaken, although I am not sure of this. He loves and understands all kinds of literature, and has been one of the chief promoters of the Royal Society. His firm friendship and his generosity in helping his friends are unexampled. In sum, he is a man rich in those moral virtues that have rendered illustrious the most revered men in Christendom—apart from his errors in religion. His whole weakness consists of a hatred, too apparent and of a completely unnecessary intensity, of Rome and the Pope. He always carries with him a catalogue of all the scriptural texts that can be stretched to consider Rome as Babylon, and the pope Anti-Christ. The King is in the habit of calling him by that name, in jest.

The Duke of Buckingham

George Villiers, second Duke of Buckingham,[47] according to the title conferred on his father by King James, of whom he was the favourite, is a man full of vices and virtues. As a young man in the King's party he was unlucky, lost his estates, and lived for a long time as a fugitive in Italy and France until his friends won Fairfax over to his cause, and demanded his restoration of Cromwell and obtained it. Fairfax gave him one of his daughters[48] for a wife, who was so ugly that later, to earn the continuance of the Duke's embraces, she has served him and still serves him as a

---

[47] The extraordinary second Duke of Buckingham (1628–1687) was certainly the most dissolute of all the dissolute courtiers of Charles II. At the same time he was a man of great intelligence and wit, who might have become an ornament to his age. Dryden, Butler, Pepys, Anthony Hamilton, and Bishop Burnet agreed about his character. Magalotti was, of course, repeating gossip about the unfortunate Duchess, who was certainly obliged to submit to the indignity of having her husband's mistresses brought to her house.

[48] Mary Fairfax (1638–1704) was the only daughter of General Thomas Fairfax.

faithful and effective procuress in the satisfaction of his highest desires.

The Duke is still very young and extremely handsome. He lives in the grand manner, dresses and dines luxuriously, plays every game very well, and is marvellously good at riding. He knows a good deal about geometry and mechanics; in philosophy he follows the experimental way and the operations of chemistry. He is very well informed about the affairs of the world and very judicious in the discussion of political matters. Courteous, affable, generous, magnanimous, he is liberal to the point of prodigality about making gifts, but tenacious to the point of meanness when it comes to paying his debts. He talks with wonderful eloquence and his persuasiveness is irresistible, fluently effective, and tactful. He is personally brave, as he has shown on many occasions and lately in the famous duel[49] with the Earl of Shrewsbury, who, in fact, died of his wound. To sum it up he is adored by the people and liked and applauded by the nobility.

On the other hand he is an atheist, a blasphemer, violent, cruel, and infamous for his licentiousness, in which he is so wrapped up that there is no sex, nor age, nor condition of persons who are spared from it. But his instincts take him to the vilest embraces, so that the most unhealthy brothels are his favourite haunts, and the most rascally lackeys his most cherished delights. From the one and the other he has therefore had an infinite harvest of the pox. Nature, who perhaps foresaw that this lord would abandon himself to the most unbridled sensuality, sought to render him unable to have intercourse with males so cleverly as to make him as much more proper and agreeable to the ladies. But it is clear that this did not serve, for without any decent considera- tion he allowed himself to think of other men, as is well known to a male dancer who was finally prevented from exercising his art for some time, and a poor French lackey who, reduced to a state of poverty so that he had to be put in the public hospitals, was found one morning in a London street with his throat cut.

They say that at present the Duke is doing no more than taking his revenge for what was done to him when he was very young, but with this difference, that nobody ever did anything to

---

[49] Buckingham had seduced the Countess of Shrewsbury, and was chal- lenged by the Earl. In more than one passage of the *Relazione* Magalotti makes it clear that he regards duelling as an honourable test of courage.

him that he did not want, while he often does to others what they do not wish for.

On the subject of courage, only once did he give reason for wonder with his unnecessary tolerance. The King was going to meet his sister, the Princess Royal, who was coming from Holland, and remounted his horse at some place or other where because of the dearth of mounts many had to be carried on exhausted beasts. Prince Rupert arrived and, seeing the Duke of Buckingham already remounted on a fresh horse without being civil enough to offer it to him, accused the Duke, tactfully at first, of lack of courtesy. The Duke answered, instead, in such a way as to irritate him extremely. Becoming enraged, the Prince seized his arm, pulled him to the ground, got on the horse and went forward. At that time the Duke had really lost the use of his right arm, and as the King immediately cooled him down, he could not reasonably pursue the quarrel. Everyone thought that after some time had passed he could find a new one, the more so as he had fought Sir James Livingstone, now the Earl of Newburgh, in France, and Prince Rupert's brother, Prince Edward, so that nobody could allege that it would be improper for him to send a challenge to a cousin of the King. One ought not to wrong the courage of the Duke for this, who had proved himself with distinction for the slightest of reasons, the greater part of his complaints resulting from love and jealousy. We can say nothing other than on this occasion he was mistaken in the choice of a decision that was too respectful towards his prince.

The Archbishop of Canterbury and the Bishop of Rochester

Gilbert, Archbishop of Canterbury,[50] is of very ordinary birth, as are most of the bishops in England. He is a man of great refinement, of much talent and brains; externally all mildness and internally all malice. He was a friend of the Chancellor and endeavoured to support him in the eyes of the King; because of this he is not now in good odour at court. He lives well, keeps a rich

---

[50] Gilbert Sheldon (1598–1677), Archbishop of Canterbury from 1663 until his death. Besides building the Sheldonian theatre at Oxford entirely at his own expense, he contributed largely to the rebuilding of St. Paul's. He discharged his official duties with assiduity and charity, remaining at Lambeth during the plague. But he was a High-Church Tory, which did not endear him to the court.

table, and lives pleasurably in his palace and garden of Lambeth on the other side of the river. At Oxford he is building, at his own expense, a magnificent theatre in solid stone, to accommodate the closing exercises that are at present held in the university church. I believe that this may be accounted the most zealous and apostolic action of this prelate, who is, however, like all the others in that country. A well-informed person has told me that without a beard it would not really be thought very safe to be with him.

Now that I am speaking of ecclesiastics, I shall say a word about the Bishop of Rochester,[51] who became famous a short time ago because of a lively attempt that he made to put his hand into the opening in the front of the hose of Lord Mohun, a boy on account of his age, but not on account of the beauty of his face, who is apt to confirm the evil interpretation given to the intentions of this prelate. The result is that the poor man is in a very miserable state because of the universal scandal that the indiscreet gossip of this young man has sown among that Presbyterian rabble, who have not only acted to have him dismissed from the office that he had, of being one of the attending bishops at the chair of the King in chapel, but want to make him lose his church. It is quite true that if he had not been a close friend of the Chancellor, the thing would not have been publicly known as much as it has; and they tell me that it is a fact, that this is not the first sign that there has been of the inclinations of this prelate. However, the thing is there, and from this standpoint he is paying more for his steadfast-ness to an old friend than for his fragility towards the young man. In this connection, a ridiculous answer was given by a solemn Presbyterian in Parliament to a brother of this bishop. The Act of Comprehension was being discussed, and the Presbyterian pro-

---

[51] John Dolben (1625–1686) was consecrated Bishop of Rochester on November 25, 1666. He later (1683) became Archbishop of York. On December 30, 1667 Sir George Cartaret told Samuel Pepys "That they do now all they can to vilify the Clergy, and do accuse Rochester (Dolben), of his being given to boys and of his putting his hand into a gentleman (who now comes to bear evidence against him) his codpiece while they were at table together." (*Diary*, ed. R. Latham and W. Matthews, 10 vols. [London, 1960–1974], vol. 8, p. 596.) The editors refer to *BM*, Add. MS 36916, f. 56r: "There is a very foul story about town of his being too familiar with the Lord Mohun, but is supposed false, the King having questioned him about it, and he denies it utterly and is so much troubled at it that he can hardly eat or drink." Magalotti is correct in his explanation of the spreading of such attacks on the bishops. The Lord Mohun referred to is Charles Mohun, Baron Mohun of Okehampton (ca. 1645–1677). The editors of *CP* describe him as "a drunken, worthless, brawl-ing fellow."

tested that the Catholics ought not to be excluded, maintaining this with effective reasons. When he had finished the Protestant said to the man beside him, but in such a way that it could be overheard, "It seems that this man has the pope in his body." The Presbyterian rose. "Certainly," he replied, "I'd much rather have the pope in my body than the bishop in my backside."

The Earl of Manchester

The Earl of Manchester,[52] Lord Chamberlain to the King, subordinate to the Earl of Lindsey[53] the Lord Great Chamberlain, is the true picture of indolence, and really nobody can be sorry for himself if, after having seen his face, he thinks otherwise. To describe him in a few words, he also put himself on the King's side when he could do no less; he was the very first to separate himself from the father.[54]

If he is an honest man he is very unfortunate because, although his words, his gestures, and his smiles are all sweetness, innocence, and humility, no one believes him and, indeed, everybody seems persuaded that he is one of the most cunning men in the world and that there is nothing in that head except making money in any way he can. The King gives him everything that he asks for, although with great reluctance. If the Earl knows this it does not offend him; he willingly takes what he gets, and after getting one thing he asks for another, and when he has obtained that, he begins again at the beginning.

The Duke of Ormonde

James Butler,[55] Duke of Ormonde, Lord-Lieutenant of Ireland, ingratiated himself with the King during his misfortunes,

---

[52] Edward Montagu, second Earl of Manchester (1602–1671). The general opinion of his contemporaries was that he was "of a generous and gentle disposition" (*DNB*). Although he detested conflict he had been involved in public affairs for most of his life.

[53] Robert Bertie, third Earl of Lindsey (ca. 1630–1701).

[54] I.e. from Charles I. As Viscount Mandeville he had been impeached in January 1642.

[55] James Butler, twelfth Earl and first Duke of Ormonde (1610–1688). Magalotti is right about the very great financial advantages that he derived from his offices, but entirely wrong about his character, which was sharply at variance with the deviousness and licentiousness of the court. At the time of Magalotti's visit Buckingham was agitating for an impeachment. On this visit Magalotti cannot have met Ormonde, who arrived in London from Ireland only on May 6, 1668.

even though in council and in the management of things public
and private he showed himself on every occasion to be a man of
little intelligence and mediocre sagacity. He was a soldier in
Ireland, France, and England, and everywhere left behind little
reputation for courage. Returning with the King, he was almost
the only one of his servants who received favours, being promptly
rewarded with the title of Duke and with the office of Lord Steward
of the household, and finally Lord-Lieutenant of Ireland, which is
the highest rank, both for dignity and for emoluments, that any
Christian prince in Europe confers on one of his servants. In all
these offices the Duke has shown infinite venality, if we consider
that in the six years that he has been in Ireland, against the
fundamental principle of not letting the lord-lieutenant take root
there for more than the first three years, he is about to bring back
60,000 pounds sterling. Great were the complaints and cries of the
people, but the force of favour sustained him. It is thought that he
is not on the point of being confirmed in the office for a third time,
but that in exchange he is to be given that of Lord High Treasurer,
at present vacant because of the death of the Earl of Southampton,[56] although the Bishop of London, Lord Ashley, and Lord
Holles all aspire to it. At the moment the treasury is administered
by five commissioners appointed by the King: the General,[57] Lord
Ashley, Sir Thomas Clifford, Sir William Coventry, and Sir John
Duncombe, a protégé of the Earl of Arlington.

Lord Robartes

Lord John Robartes,[58] Lord Privy Seal, is one of those men
who have got it into their heads to see how well a lazy man can
really live. He comes from the lowest class, for his father was a
tanner who, having made a very great deal of money from his
trade, was lucky enough to be able to help King James in a time of
need, and was repaid by being knighted and made a baron.

Then this son of his, having become the brother-in-law of
Manchester, because the first wives of both were sisters, continued

---

[56] Thomas Wriothesley, fourth Earl of Southampton (1607–1667).

[57] General George Monk, Duke of Albemarle.

[58] Lord John Robartes (1606–1685), was Lord Privy Seal at the time of
Magalotti's visit. His father, Richard Robartes, had made his fortune in wool
and tin, not in tanning. Lord John was indeed the brother-in-law of the Earl of
Manchester through his second wife, but Magalotti's description of their
campaign together is a figment of someone's imagination. It is generally agreed
that in later life Lord Robartes was far from energetic.

to seek his fortune at the time of the revolution, not in favour of King or Parliament, although he and Manchester had been among the originators of the revolt, but forming a third party, ready to help either of the other two, according to what they could get out of it. Meanwhile, having retired into the County of Cornwall, where because of the location of their estates they are, so to speak, the rulers, and have a very great authority and following, they then raised a small body of armed men under the command of Manchester (the same man that I discussed above) with Robartes as his lieutenant. It never saw the faces of an enemy, and the men were dispersed after a short time. Meanwhile, enlightened by this and other events, they applied themselves seriously to establishing themselves in the King's party and to working for his restoration, negotiating with him (like all the others) for large and hidden rewards. They did very well out of this, and Robartes got the privy seal, a very important office in England because there had to pass through his hands all the documents about personal favours, those that do not go down in perpetuity in families, as the latter have to pass under the great seal of the kingdom. From this it is very easy to understand the two main ways in which this office is desirable, for it necessarily carries with it a constant access to the King, and the rewards and "gifts" of all those who receive favours. These latter the Lord Privy Seal can assess at his discretion. But he availed himself of the first prerogative with great moderation and disdained the second entirely; some say not because of any virtue in him, but because he abandons himself to his own pleasures and forgets and neglects his own affairs, although in other ways he is a subtle and clever man and manages to keep on good terms with the other principal ministers.

It is quite true that he almost always lives at Chelsea, in one of his houses about a mile from London. Concerning his laziness, they say that two years ago,[59] at the news that a Dutch fleet had come into the river [Medway] as far as Chatham, the King wished to call a meeting of the council, and sent for him at a somewhat unusual hour; but he refused to interrupt his game of bowls in order to come. His disposition is obstinate, proud, unrefined, and

---

[59] The Dutch attack on Chatham took place in June, 1667, only a few months before Magalotti's visit to London, so that it is unlikely that he would misremember the date. This would confirm Miss Crinò's contention (*Edizione critica*, p. 8) that the *Relazione* was written in 1669 from notes taken early in 1668.

indiscreet. He is greedy for food, tobacco, and wine; a great lover of women, and fond only of idleness and the comforts of life.

Not so is his son.[60] He is a knowing, courteous, prudent, and spruce young man, who is already making a very good name for himself in the lower House. The story of his marriage is very curious. On his return from his journey to Italy he began to frequent the wife of a certain Bodville in her house. She had formerly been the mistress of Cromwell, and a number of soldiers desired her affection. She left her husband or, to put it more correctly, he himself went away, declaring that the second of the two very lovely daughters that she had was not his. Young Robartes, now almost part of that household, where life went on with a freedom suitable to a brothel, fell madly in love with this second daughter, against whom, besides the unfavourable conjectures about her as the daughter of such a mother, also militated various bits of gossip aroused by the passion that three young noblemen had for her, more particularly the Earl of Chesterfield.[61] Nevertheless he married her. His father was furious and would not see him for three or four years, and his father-in-law likewise would hear nothing about it. The young man, desperate, got on his horse one day and went away to Cornwall where his father was, threw himself at his feet, showed him the portrait of his wife, and said that this woman was the cause of his fault. The old fellow, who after all had not a heart of stone, looked at it and looked at it again, was touched, pardoned the young man entirely, and from that time on was once more at peace with him. Thus when the son had gone back home to his wife, and the father had been remarried to a young and lovely lady,[62] they found the means of staying on good terms (some people say) because of the prudence of the father and the tact of the son. They next became reconciled to the wife's father,[63] and in this way: he would leave this daughter his fortune, the other already having died, and Robartes would pay so much a year to him and so much (if I am not mistaken) to the mother-in-law, even though she was divorced, obligating himself further to pay him a thousand pounds a year for the maintenance of his wife and himself. It is true that on his death this man appointed someone else as his heir, leaving his daughter only four thousand

---

[60] Robert Robartes, who married Sarah, daughter of John Bodville.
[61] Philip Stanhope, second Earl of Chesterfield (1633–1713).
[62] Letitia Isabella, daughter of a Sir John Smith, of Kent.
[63] This was Thomas Wynne.

pounds for her lawful portion. This daughter was made to appear of age by the omnipotence of [Sir Heneage] Finch,[64] who moved heaven and earth in this case, and the second will was declared invalid, so that Robartes has entered into possession of the whole inheritance, which must be about two thousand a year. He will have about sixty thousand crowns of his own.

Father and son are Presbyterians and both very jealous,[65] perhaps because they know what sort of women they have on their hands. The mother lost her nose because of a certain malady, went to France to be cured, and came back with a false nose so elegantly fitted that with all the fifty years that she has on her shoulders she looks like a fresh and lovely woman.

The Earl of Lauderdale

John, Earl of Lauderdale,[66] a Scotsman, the King's Secretary for Scottish affairs; one could call him the serpent among the eels, and all his sorrow consists in being too well known. His natural talents are great, his way of operating extremely able; no one is more resourceful than he, and he is the most proper man to form parties and destroy them according to his own purposes. In his hands is all the manoeuvering of the religion and the special interests of his country, and because his office brings him an intimate access to the King, it gives him the opportunity of introducing his principles and of testing the effectiveness of his talents. It is said that this is much more often to the disadvantage of his enemies, and perhaps sometimes of uninterested people, than to the advantage of his friends. Everyone wishes him ill and he wishes well to few. His usual occupation is smoking and drinking, but neither tobacco nor wine ever stop his polemics. In fact he uses drunkenness in order to get on better with the King, who takes

---

[64] Sir Heneage Finch (1621–1682), then (1664) Solicitor General. See Pepys' *Diary,* ed. H. B. Wheatley (London, 1924), vol. 4, pp. 117–18, and note. The case of Robartes vs. Wynne finally went to the House of Lords, who threw it back to the Court of Chancery, which finally decided in favour of Thomas Wynne. (*Reports in Chancery,* 15 Car. 2, fol. 434), so that Magalotti's conclusion is contrary to what finally happened.

[65] Lord Robartes' jealousy of the Duke of York—apparently justified—is amusingly described in Anthony Hamilton, *Memoirs of the Comte de Gramont,* tr. Peter Quennell (London, 1930), pp. 167–68.

[66] John Maitland, Earl (later Duke) of Lauderdale (1616–1682), was an able, dissolute, and unscrupulous man who kept his great influence on both the King and the Duke of York almost to the end of his life.

delight in his conversation, especially when he sees him in such a state. He is aware that he serves as a laughing-stock, but makes others pay dearly for the entertainment that they get from him; indeed he makes a business out of making people laugh. In times past he was against the King,[67] and a long imprisonment gave him a knowledge of history because of the assiduous reading that he began to do, and now history is the strong point of his learning, just as guile and subterfuge are those of his ability and, it may be said, of his present fortune.

Lord Ashley

They say that Lord Ashley Cooper[68] is of very obscure birth, having been enriched by an inheritance from someone of the same name. He began hypocritically to make himself necessary to the managers of the disturbances. He changed sides many times with the wind and was always unfaithful to everyone until, having made himself necessary to the King in his restoration, he received for this last service the reward that he did not deserve for his past conduct. He has now been made a baron and Peer of the Realm, a member of the Privy Council and Chancellor of the Exchequer—the finest office in England for a thief—and he has a hundred other offices that have made him rich. A cunning man, who pretends to be simple and is not, pretends to be a friend to everyone and is a friend to nobody, he has honeyed words and most evil deeds. He has none of the polish of erudition and no ability that transcends his experience in the ordinary business of the kingdom, as he has never gone into the management of foreign affairs. He is a Presbyterian, and his greatest talent is in introducing a piece of business and bringing it to a conclusion according to his intention, not at all by any superiority of mind but by a prodigious abundance of subterfuges, lies, votes, and private intrigues. He has had two wives; the one that he has now is beautiful and natural in every way. He has one son who, they say, is now being married.

---

[67] He had been a Covenanter and a Scottish representative to the Westminster Assembly during the Civil War.

[68] Anthony Ashley Cooper, Lord Ashley (1621–1683), later the first Earl of Shaftesbury, has suffered more than most of his contemporaries from vituperation, from which this account by Magalotti does nothing to rescue him. One may perhaps point out a few matters in which our author is wrong: Lord Ashley's father was a knight and he inherited large estates; his first principle was always the supremacy of Parliament; and lastly, in that corrupt age he never used his offices to enrich himself, either in money or land.

The Earl of Anglesey

Arthur, Earl of Anglesey,[69] is a man who, between nature and the gout, has become a ridiculous figure, and cannot be said to be either healthy or crippled. He is tall, has short curly hair, the scalp almost bald, his face is long and emaciated, his complexion between purple and green, his eyes frightening; he keeps his mouth open as if he always wanted to laugh, although he never does. He is reputed to be a man of very little talent, untruthful, avaricious, deceitful, who has been lacerated by the populace in all his offices, and is thought to be entirely without religion; one who has never served the King except when he could do no less and when he has believed that it would be useful to him.

The great lustre of his family begins in him, and in a short time his wealth has also become very great. The treasury of Ireland, administered by him for many years, can bear strong witness to this. Now the King has made him exchange this office for that of Treasurer of the Navy in place of Sir George Cartaret,[70] having been induced to remove the latter in order to answer the loud complaints of the soldiers and sailors of the fleet who, impelled by the hunger that the avarice of this man was making them suffer, have several times been on the point of throwing him in the sea or cutting his throat on land, which they would have done if people in his party had not come to his aid. Parliament likewise was against him and wanted to proceed with a rigorous audit of the accounts of the immense sums that passed through his hands during the last war; so much so, that not less for the first reason than for the second, it was advisable for the King to remove him from his former office, sending him instead (so much can these people do with this poor prince) to dissipate the inheritance of another kingdom.[71]

Two Knights

Sir William Morice,[72] Secretary of State, in the same line as Lord Arlington, is a decrepit old man, extremely skilful at busi-

---

[69] Arthur Annesley, first Earl of Anglesea (1614–1686). There is no question that he made a great deal of money from his offices, but he was certainly a useful and able man.

[70] Pepys was told of this by Sir George Cartaret on June 18, 1667. The affairs of the navy were in a dreadful state at this time. Anglesea lost the office again in November, 1668.

[71] Sir George became Deputy Treasurer of Ireland and held this post until 1673.

[72] Sir William Morice (1602–1676) was related to Monck and had helped

ness, who at times has been of importance at court, but now that his colleague is in favour he has become quite obscure and of no esteem, and it is left to him barely to perform his duties in matters of no consequence.

Sir [William] Coventry,[73] of the Williams family,[74] is the younger son of a Lord Coventry who was once treasurer of the kingdom. He is a well-bred man and a lover of literature, and shows great affability. In years gone by, after having travelled over a great part of Europe, he came back to England at the beginning of the civil wars and became involved in affairs. In all the negotiations that he had, first against the King[75] and then in his favour, he acquired a reputation for prudence. At first he served in the post of Secretary of the Duke in the navy, and was liked by the Duke better than anyone else. But now he is in disgrace for having entered into a clique with Lord Arlington, the Duke of Buckingham, and other enemies of the Chancellor in order to ruin him. He is considered a man of ability but with little courage and low-spirited, although to tell the truth he has never done anything to get such a reputation. His aim is to become Secretary of State one day.[76] His blemishes are hypocrisy and ingratitude.

Lord Holles

Denzil, Lord Holles,[77] is the brother of an earl and thus of noble birth, as they say in England. In his youth he was always busy with love-affairs and negotiations. He has travelled all over the world, and is very knowledgeable about countries, customs, and foreign affairs. Elected to the House of Commons in 1640, he was one of the chief leaders of the rebels and one of the fiercest enemies of that poor prince, who, wishing to ruin him before his own fall, saw all the common people of London rise up to shield him from his revenge.[78] Holles, later recognizing that fortune was

---

in the restoration of the King. The "colleague" was Arlington. He left public life in 1668 and retired to his estate.

[73] Sir William Coventry (ca. 1627–1686), fourth son of Thomas, first Baron Coventry (1578–1640), who was Lord Keeper to Charles I.

[74] *Della casa Willielms.* This is entirely obscure.

[75] He seems, in fact, to have been abroad during the interregnum.

[76] It is possible that Magalotti was confusing him with his elder brother, Henry (1619–1686), who did become Secretary of State in 1672.

[77] Denzil Holles (1599–1680) had been created Baron Holles in 1661. He was politically active for over half a century, and one of the leading parliamentary opponents of Cromwell in the last years of the Protectorate.

[78] This may refer to an occasion in 1642 when Holles, with several other

not by a wide margin maintaining her promises to him in the Republican government, having lived for some time repenting of his machinations, and being reduced to living suspected by Cromwell and the government, succeeded in putting himself in the service of the King again. Sent to France with the title of ambassador he demonstrated, as much in that embassy as in one at Breda, that he had a subtle mind, rich in alternatives and expedients, and able in the management of great affairs. His manner is natural, and too respectful rather than discourteous. His generosity and magnificence are those of a prince rather than of a private nobleman. He is beginning to look old, but neither years nor concerns have ever been able to take the gallantry from his mind.

The Earl of St. Albans

Henry Jermyn, Earl of St. Albans,[79] the youngest son in his family, which was not very large, was a page in the presence chamber of the Queen-Mother of England. He was an extremely handsome young man, and for that reason was always pleasing to the ladies. As the first fruit of some budding affection or other he was made a knight errant, then a lover; as a lover he followed the adverse fortunes of his lady with great constancy. When this affair was over, he attained the title of Baron and finally the office of Lord Chamberlain to the Queen, which he still holds. He is a splendid, fortunate, and liberal man; a gambler; all in all, a man who has the favour of the courtiers but is not esteemed by the soldiers or by the ministers, the former prejudiced against him because of some happening or other, the latter for his handling of the last negotiations between England and France before the recent war, all of which passed through his hands. At present he is out of favour at court, both Baron Lisola[80] and the Spanish ambassador[81] having contributed to discrediting him, making people recognize him for what he in fact is, a man who is wholly devoted to French interests and who acts with no other purpose than to promote the vast projects of that crown at whatever cost to England. But without a courtier's ambition, he finds enough to live on, abundantly con-

members of Parliament who had been impeached, took refuge in the city of London, and later returned in triumph to Westminster (*DNB*).

[79] Henry Jermyn, Earl of St. Albans (d. 1684). By and large, Magalotti's thumbnail sketch is as just as it is incomplete.

[80] See note 91 below, p. 63.

[81] See note 87 below, p. 62.

tented with his pleasures and amusements, to both of which he is extraordinarily attached; and the Queen-Mother's purse, always open to meet all his wishes, amply provides the means of satisfaction. He begins to show his age and is very corpulent, but for all this one can still recognize in his face the traces of marvellous good looks.

Sir Samuel Morland

Sir Samuel Morland[82] is a man who because of a certain extraordinary ability in arithmetic, in mechanics, and in cryptography is held in some esteem by the King. He was a student in the University of Cambridge when Cromwell chanced to be impressed by his talent and drew him into his orbit in order to have a pupil. Every day his confidence in him and his affection for him increased, so that he made him aware of his business. When the understanding of the young man had been matured by this experience and illuminated by these words of wisdom he was sent to Turin as Resident, from where he went to Geneva with the title of ambassador to that republic, in order to accredit the false zeal of his master by specious ostentation.

Returning to England by way of France, he bound himself verbally to the father of a young lady of Normandy, a Huguenot—with whom he had decided to fall in love on the strength of a description of her that he had had from her cousin at Geneva—to come back and marry her; and although he had to go across the Channel at that time because of the haste Cromwell was in, nevertheless the nuptials took place in less than a year. At this time he had a salary of more than three thousand pounds a year, with the promise that he would be promoted to the office of Secretary of State at the death of the incumbent. Meanwhile his wife had acquired a great power over her husband, and this moved Henry Howard[83] of Norfolk to make use of this means of drawing him into the King's party. When the woman changed, the man did also, and from that time on nothing ever came to his notice

---

[82] Sir Samuel Morland (1625–1695). Magalotti's opinion of him is that of his contemporaries. Before his death in 1695 Morland became extraordinarily pious. For a long time in the 1670s Cosimo III tried to persuade him to move to Florence. See Anna Maria Crinò, "I rapporti di Sir Samuel Morland con Cosimo III dei Medici," in her *Fatte e figure del seicento anglo-toscano* (Florence, 1957), pp. 213–59.

[83] Henry Howard (1628–1684), later sixth Duke of Norfolk. See also p. 115 below.

with which, at an infinite risk, he did not acquaint the King, up to the point of saving his life and that of his brother, the Duke, who were to be killed in the house of a traitor near London.[84] This man had been won over by the partisans of the King, to receive him secretly in his house in company with the Duke; but considering the high price he could get for these two princes, he called on Sir Samuel and when a price of forty thousand pounds had been agreed upon, disclosed the matter to him. Sir Samuel at once sent off information about this to the King, who had not as yet crossed the sea, and then went to inform Cromwell of his negotiation with this fine fellow. This was very well received, but the caution of the princes, who had been warned in advance, caused the expectations of the protector to be deceived.

After Cromwell's death and the divisions within the army, Sir Samuel began to see that the purposes of Monk were favourable to the King. But Monk knew the weakness of his troops, and that if they had to fight Lambert and [Fleetwood][85] they would be beaten without any doubt, so when he could he sowed such distrust and intimated such mutual jealousy between the two captains, formerly closely united, that not only were their forces weakened, but their troops even began to decay and indeed to disband, to the advantage of those of Monk. The populace came to trust his forces and began to shout "Long live the King!" throughout the kingdom.

A few days before the King was recalled, the Chancellor wanted to make an infallible test of Morland's feelings towards him, and he did it like this: he wrote him a letter in the ordinary cipher of the King and in the name of the King himself, in which he asked him, in completion of so many and so important services rendered, that he should tell him plainly how his Chancellor had behaved, and how much he could promise himself about his fidelity in future. Sir Samuel, who would rather be faithful to the King than to the minister, replied that as to his fidelity he had always found the Chancellor very honest; however, he did not think him the greatest politician in the world, and he would have wished that he might speak more circumspectly, not because he had ever failed, but only on the consideration that silence is the soul of great affairs. He said this because the Chancellor, the

---

[84] This is usually referred to as Sir Richard Willis's plot. However, the way in which it was foiled by Morland was quite unlike Magalotti's story.

[85] A lacuna in the MS. I owe this suggestion to Professor Trimble.

emptiest braggart in his every thought, as soon as he conceived of something advantageous to the King, was induced by his thirst for applause to take so many people into his confidence that sooner or later he stumbled on to one of Cromwell's spies, and the beautiful design vanished. Now, having found out about Morland in this way, and having assured himself by some trick that he would not go and speak to the King about this matter, the Chancellor never pardoned him. The knight tried to excuse himself in a letter by confessing the fact and justifying himself, but the Chancellor kept on laughing and deceiving him. It is enough to say that his reward ended with the title of baronet and a pension of five hundred pounds.

His temperament is melancholy and a little queer, and his machines have given room to his competitors to discredit him with the King, making him pass for a philosopher,[86] so that apart from being amused by these curious things, the King holds him in little esteem. In truth his talent for politics is not wonderful.

Ambassadors at the Court

Don Antonio Messia de Tovar y Paz,[87] Count of Molina, Spanish ambassador at the Court of England, is a very fine gentleman in respect to his affability, politeness, generosity, and courtesy; but being a minister is not his proper calling, because even though he seeks by hard work and diligence to make up for what he cannot attain to with the advantages of great courage and with a certain superiority to business, yet something more is needed, particularly in a court where, because of the division of authority between the prince and his subjects, an active and manipulative mind is required. His calling has always been in the affairs of the

---

[86] In a letter to Cardinal Leopold, written from Paris on June 29, 1668 (*BNCF*, MS Gal. 278, 185r–186r), Magalotti gives an explanation of this remark: "I could never tell Your Highness how prejudicial it is for a man of fashion from that side of the mountains to pass for a philosopher and mathematician. The ladies at once believe that he must be enamoured of the moon, or Venus, or some silly thing like that. To show that this is true, Dr. Bernadin Guasconi, who is no fool, began to be jealous of me in the house of a certain widow in London, where he had introduced me. He merely told the lady that I was a philosopher, and it was as so much poison to me, for from that time on I was considered a platonic lover, and in consequence I could bring nothing to a conclusion other than to admire *the high first cause* in her external beauty." This letter was published by A. Fabroni, *Lettere inedite d'uomini illustri*, 2 vols. (Florence, 1773 and 1775), vol. 1, pp. 307–309. Fabroni added the emphasis.

[87] He was ambassador of Spain at the English court from 1665 until 1669.

royal administration, and when he moved to England he left Brussels where he exercised the office of *veidore*,[88] which he held for many years. Indeed, the sole reason for sending him to London was to have in that post a person accepted by the King and deserving a great deal from him, considering the important services that he had rendered him by lending him large sums of money when he lived in Flanders merely as a poor and private nobleman.

The Count is small in stature and full of life and has a very white face. His age would seem to be little over forty. He has an ugly wife. He lives most nobly, entertains, and is infinitely respectful and courteous towards everyone, which has gained him universal favour in the court. He has a defect or infirmity, usually attributed by the doctors to the sublimation of hypochondriacal vapours,[89] which very often obliges him to close his left eye very tightly and to twist his mouth in that direction. This deforms his face strangely, making him appear apoplectic.

On Count Dohna,[90] the ambassador of Sweden, I gave a report last winter while I was at The Hague, where he was in the same post of ambassador to the States-General. For that reason I shall not discuss him, and shall pass to the Baron de Lisola,[91] envoy extraordinary from the emperor. This most worthy man has no need to be introduced nor to be praised by me, as he has made himself notable enough with his writings and his negotiations in all the courts of Europe. Nevertheless it might perhaps be said that his missions have been of ill omen to all those princes to whom he has gone as a minister, for there are even those who attribute to his negotiations the extreme peril of Denmark in the siege of Copenhagen, and the invasion of Poland.

He is a man who, to judge by his appearance, is not far from sixty years old;[92] of medium height, his face and figure emaciated and rather sad and dismal in appearance. Business is his work, his

---

[88] *Veedor* is the Spanish word for "inspector."

[89] As this was most probably written after he had been to Paris, one might think that Magalotti had been to hear *Le malade imaginaire*. Unfortunately for such a hypothesis, Molière's great satire on the medical profession was first performed only in 1673.

[90] Christof Delphicus Dohna (1628–1668).

[91] François-Paul, Baron de Lisola (1613–1675), though born in France, employed his very great talents in the service of the Holy Roman Empire, and in particular against the power of his native country. The emperor sent him to England in 1643, and afterwards as imperial ambassador to Poland, Spain, and Portugal. He was a pamphleteer of note.

[92] He was fifty-five.

comfort, and his nourishment. Although he is from the Franche
Comté, he speaks four languages like a native: Spanish, French,
Italian, and German. He writes marvellously and always speaks as
he writes, soon becoming so warm in a discussion that, leaving the
form of familiar conversation and passing to argument, he brings
out his own reasons with such fine proofs and illustrates them with
such beautiful examples, that one seems to be hearing a book being
read, rather than a man speaking. But he knows his own worth,
and this is to the great detriment of anyone who is with him and is
engaged in the same business, for it is certain that he wants to have
all the merit himself. Often he disagrees too completely with his
partner in order to preserve appearances, as has now happened in
these negotiations about an alliance between England and Holland, in which the Count of Molina, with all his position as
ambassador, received the oracles of the imperial envoy, although
the interests of his master were mainly being discussed.

The Baron is a man of the greatest religious faith and of the
most burning zeal for his prince. Besides, he is an omnipotent
man, who is unbounded in the force of his words and in the
effectiveness of the plots that he invents to put them into action. In
all, he is perhaps the greatest minister that the house of Austria
has, perhaps the greatest among the princely courts of Europe. He
is married; his wife begins to be old, and although she has acquired
refinement by going with him on all his travels, to all the courts,
and even in the Polish army and to sieges where the Queen or her
husband were, with all this she has not that bearing nor that
nobility of manner that would be expected of such a woman. She
has an only daughter of great wit, who has just recently married a
Fleming, Baron Sprau, a native of Louvain, who is a young man of
seventeen and a very good horseman.

Monsieur de Ruvigny,[93] envoy extraordinary of France, is of
advanced age and a Huguenot in religion. He is very alert and
tireless in the work of the ministry. He is always everywhere and
thinks of everything, and it is difficult to conceal anything whatever from his eyes. When I was in England before,[94] the title of
French minister did not get him much favour at the court, so that

---

[93] Henri de Massue, Marquis de Ruvigny (1610–1689), was a soldier for
the first half of his life. He was ambassador or special envoy in England several
times. Upon the revocation of the edict of Nantes he took refuge in England,
became naturalized, and died at Greenwich.

[94] I.e., in 1668. This is further evidence that the *Relazione* was written
only after his visit in the suite of Prince Cosimo in 1669.

he went more willingly to the apartment of the Duchess, who still considers herself as a Frenchwoman, than to that of the Queen, and his daily conversation was in the house of the Earl of St. Albans, whom everyone calls the English ambassador of France in England. Ruvigny is courteous, wise, and calm, and in nothing but the quick way he acts can one recognize anything of the character of a Frenchman.

I shall omit the Dutch ambassadors because, as they never show themselves anywhere, I confess that I did not often remember to ask about them. It is true that as far as I have heard them casually discussed, I have found no one who has a great opinion of their adequacy, and it is certain that they do not live in a style corresponding to their post.

Foreigners at the Court

I shall now speak of some foreigners[95] whom I have found at the court. First of all I remember, as someone already established in England for several years, a certain Italian personage who calls himself one of the Ubaldini. Of his birth I know nothing, but I know very well what he has done since. At present he professes the Protestant religion, and face to face he confesses that he is an atheist. There are those who say that he has been a friar and that, leaving his order, he went to Constantinople and there, after having himself circumcised, tried his fortune with little success. After having been in various trades in different parts of Europe and in several of the courts of heretical princes, he came to London where, spreading stories about his birth and displaying some superficial learning, he obtained some grant from the King and some sort of pension from the bishops, on which he is now living. He is young, perhaps thirty-two years old, but extraordinarily fat, so that in time he will be entirely unable to move. I did not admire any very uncommon talent in him, and I particularly observed that his conversation is certainly abundant, but disordered, confused, and unsettled, always passing from one thing to another without finishing anything. His tongue wounds without mercy, and in all his talk he affects impiety and makes a show of atheism. He plumes

---

[95] Few of these people are of sufficient importance to warrant footnotes. Magalotti's omission of Bernadino Guasconi (1614–1687), naturalized as Sir Bernard Gascoigne, who performed services for three Kings of England and was elected F.R.S., can be explained by the fact that he was already well known in Tuscany.

himself on being a moral man, and I am informed that he has some sort of agreement with his friends. From what they tell me he is dedicated beyond all reason to pleasures of all kinds.[96]

Before leaving the Italians I shall speak of Marquis Gioseppe Malaspina d'Olivola,[97] brother of Marchioness Malaspina, who was maid-of-honor to the Grand Duchess of Tuscany and is now a nun among the barefooted Carmelites at Genoa. This gentleman, wishing to escape from the solitudes of Lunigiana, passed into the service of the Queen of Sweden as her groom of the chamber, shortly before she left for Rome. Going to Hamburg with her last year, he obtained leave to take the waters at Spa, from where, with more leave, he crossed to England and came to London. There, introduced into an English house, he pleased a Protestant girl and a dowry figured at 8,000 pounds pleased him, for he considered it far, far superior to what he could hope for in his own country, considering his mediocre gifts. So he began to discuss a marriage. At first the lady showed herself unwilling to abandon her religion, though not to go to Italy, so that for the maintenance of a minister and other private necessities she intended to retain some part of her dowry. To this the Marquis was almost already to consent, but when he heard the opinion of one of his friends that he should consider the commitment into which he was entering, to be obliged to keep a heretical wife in Italy, he was almost disposed to let the matter drop. I next understood that the lady resolved to become a Catholic, and there only remained the scruple about communion in both kinds, so that I am sure the marquis will fall for it. She is of gentle birth and her morals are as good as one can expect of an Englishwoman; she is very ugly and her temper is fierce rather than lively. The Marquis is a very good young man, but apart from his birth I have not noticed anything in him that is better than mediocre.

I found in London a gentleman of the Pagnini family of Lucca, a young man of about twenty-two, who had already made a grand tour through Poland and Germany, but with little profit, for he still preserves a pitiable poverty of mind.

---

[96] He had made a favourable impression on Boyle and Oldenburg, and the latter proposed his election to the Royal Society, which took place on November 28, 1667. He was quite inactive in the Society.

[97] Miss Crinò has studied the relations of the family of Giuseppe Malaspina (1633–1682) with England. See *Inediti su alcuni contatti tosco-britannico nel Seicento,* in *English Miscellany* (Rome), 1961, no. 12, p. 181.

The Marquis of Flammarens, a French nobleman from Normandy, has already been at this court for about four years, after having lost all his estates as a punishment for the duel in which he fought as a second against two brothers, the Marquises of La Frette. His first refuge was at The Hague, which he left to embark in the Dutch fleet when it went out for the first battle. When they had come within sight of the English fleet, he went over in a small boat to the flagship, where the Duke of York was. After the battle he went to London and was introduced to Lord Arlington, who got an extra 300 pounds from the King to help him. Since then he has always been at court, where he is very highly regarded by the King, who very often admits him to his dinners at the house of the Duchess of Monmouth, and sometimes to his drinking parties. It was said lately that the King had begun to be bored with him and had given him hints about this, but that the marquis pretended not to notice and the King, in his usual way, had not the heart to free himself from him by some means or other. The Marquis has indeed done what he can to re-establish himself in France, but the King has always declined to help, alleging conscientious scruples against breaking his oath not to forgive duels. The Duchess de [Chaulnes],[98] sister of those La Frette brothers, was recently thinking of interesting the Pope in taking this specious pretext away from the King. The Marquis is a very handsome nobleman; he pleases the ladies and the ladies please him. They talk about a very rich marriage with a Catholic lady. He is brave, prudent, well-mannered, and courteous; in fact he does not in any way deserve the injuries of his present disgrace.

Concerning the Marquis de Sainctot, a Frenchman, I wrote down when he arrived the reasons for his coming to England. He had aroused the indignation of the King of France and had lost his commission as lieutenant in the guards by not going to the fighting in the Franche Comté. I really do not know whether this was due to the force of maternal affection or whether it was because in the last campaign, where he had a musket-ball in the thigh, he had found that the profession of arms did not suit his temperament. It is certain that if the King gave him the time he meant to sell his commission; but now he has abandoned this idea. This young man was at Rome for some time. Everywhere wine and pleasures of all sorts have been the basis of all his thoughts, all his conversation, and all his diligence.

---

[98] Moretti's suggestion to fill a blank in the MS

M. de Beringhen, a Huguenot Frenchman, of very modest birth but the son of a very rich father, was in England for some months. He is a young man of about twenty-five, preparing himself for the Bar by legal studies. He came here to the court immediately after the treaty of Breda in the retinue of Monsieur de Ruvigny, where he was made aware of many secret proceedings. He is estimable for his curiosity and diligence in profiting from his travels, but ridiculously mean, and intolerable in his presumptuous vanity and effrontery, letting it be understood, as he says everywhere, that by his wise conduct and tactful moderation he has re-established the fame of France and, if this is possible, conquered the natural dislike of the French nation in England.

In the company of Count Dohna there is also, first of all, a nephew who has the same surname. This is a young man aged twenty-four, handsome, but his good looks have not the slightest alloy of nobility of manner nor pride of spirit. But nevertheless he is full of vanity and thinks he has all the ladies of the court sighing for him. The King is kind to him and so he finds kindness in the houses of the Duke and the Duchess. I have had little conversation with him, but in that little I have found him most impertinent and overbearing. He likes to begin discussions about religion and affects great disdain for Catholics.

The Count of Brederode, also a Dutchman, nephew of the ambassador, is a true Dutchman, rough, disorderly, uncivil and absent-minded, if not scatter-brained. His love-affair with a widow, and seeing his cousin get ahead of him in the favour of the King, keep him in great anxiety and melancholy.

Baron Spran, a young Swede of a very noble family but of very mediocre ability, does not surpass with any rare mental gifts the usual imperfections of his tender age.

Count Wrangel, the only son of the Constable, will, I hear, be dead in a few days. There is no doubt that his poor father will be inconsolable for this loss, for his magnanimous spirit drew a strong nourishment from the life of this son, for whom he had great hopes. But it is true that if one considers this young man without the father's passion one can very easily find reasons for consolation; because his spirit, not less wild than his eyes, nor his mind, no less strange than his person, promised no higher or nobler inclinations than those that at a tender age had planted such deep roots in his heart; these were drunkenness, the brothel, gambling, and sometimes blasphemy. Somehow it would have been more tolerable if his brain had always been in the same state, but I hear that it sometimes became confused and clouded.

Finally I will name Count Gustavus Adolphus de la Gardie,[99] eldest son of the Grand Chancellor of Sweden; in two months of continuous conversation that very soon became close and trusting friendship, I have never been able to find any other imperfection than an exceeding delicacy and too steadfast diligence in the matter of honour. This could even be turned into a virtue if it all arose in him by conscious choice, without being at all influenced by a serious, melancholy, and solitary temperament. Apart from this, his courtesy, virginal modesty, attention, punctuality, kindness, and self-possession are accompanied by the most respectful consideration. His obvious frankness, his noble curiosity, erudition, and delight in all beautiful things; his affection, his prudence, and the maturity of his conversation and his observations made me esteem this gentleman so greatly that I am repaying his friendship with some of the main acquisitions that I feel able to bring back from my travels. I have news that he is at present in Holland to begin his tour through Germany and from there to come to Italy and be at Florence during the next summer.

---

[99] Gustavus Adolphus de la Gardie (1647–1695). This young man was a guest of the Royal Society on February 27/March 8, 1667/8, when Magalotti and Falconieri were also present (Birch, *History*, 2, 252).

Intrigues at the Court of
England

Now that I come to speak of the intrigues at the English court I
have to establish a rule, for the truth or falsehood of which I cannot
answer at this time. True or false, it was certainly put to me as
indubitable. The rule is that in all the Court of England there was
not at that time any honest woman except the Queen, but she was
universally reputed to be weak and not very clever. But let them
say what they like, all these malicious people, who do not believe
that virtue has anything to do with these things, but attribute all
virtuous abstinence from indulgence in pleasures either to poverty
of spirit or to a frigid disposition. It must be remembered that the
Queen of England is from Portugal, and among the Portuguese she
can be considered rather to have an extraordinarily hot and dry
temperament; and this is because she has such a superabundance of
blood, and so effervescent is it, that she is very often subjected to
extraordinary purges, which may perhaps be harmful to her fecundity, as I indicated in another place while speaking of her in these
memoirs. It is true that she drinks nothing but water, but what she
gains by this she loses seven times over by the immoderate use of
powdered spices in her food, and ambergris and musk in confec-
tionery. But if all these things should be insufficient to confirm her
virtue, the self-control that she exercises in the embraces of her
husband would itself be irrefutable evidence of it, and prove
conclusively that she is more than usually sensitive to pleasure. She
finds the King provided by nature with implements most suitable
for exciting it, and it is said that her ecstasy is then so extreme that
after the ordinary escape of those humours that the violence of
pleasure presses even from women, blood comes from her genital
parts in such great abundance that it does not stop for several days.
With all this, it may be as much because of her care not to harm her
chance of bearing children that she very often refuses the embraces
of the King, who sleeps with her every night; and when she does
get ready to receive them, she prepares herself with an unusual
diet, and in the act itself she manages to avoid all those refinements

that others seek in order to stimulate more vehemently the heat of wantonness.

In spite of this there is no lack of people who think that she is swayed by affection, and who interpret as the effect of amorous inclination all the demonstrations of courtesy and familiarity with which she distingushes from all the others Lord Ossory,[1] son of the Duke of Ormonde. This opinion is insulting not only to the virtue of the Queen, but also to her good taste, for this nobleman is not as suitable for the lover of a great princess as for an innocent friend, while, apart from being rather ugly, he is also married. I have spoken of this in order not to conceal anything that is being said; but to do the same for what is believed, it is proper to say that among people with common sense there is no one at the court who does not believe this to be a slander and who does not admit and admire in the highest degree the wise moderation of this good and virtuous princess.

The King is not as scrupulous, and his long-continued affair with Madam Castlemaine[2] is already well known in every part of Europe. This woman is in a position that cannot hide her very bad qualities. She was born a Protestant and has prostitution bred into her by ancient inheritance in the maternal line. Before coming into the hands of the King she passed through those of many men, and among the others the Duke of Buckingham with all his relations were not the last to avail themselves of her. When the King came to desire her she at once abandoned herself to his pleasures with almost no resistance. Lord Gerard,[3] who at that time held the privy purse and slept in the King's chamber, had the first information about this, for the King at first had her come to his bedroom, before he gave her apartments in the palace. One night he was in a terrible quandary when in bed with her, for a fire broke out near his room, and they found themselves surrounded by the guards and all the court, who had run to extinguish it. Meanwhile the lady was in the King's bed, and he found it advisable to put her, naked, into the hands of Gerard, who thought of a place to stow her safely

---

[1] Thomas Butler, Earl of Ossory (1634–1680).

[2] Barbara Villiers, Countess of Castlemaine (1641–1709), later Duchess of Cleveland in her own right. Charles acknowledged the paternity of five of her children. Her amours were notorious, and she was not at all faithful to the King. None of the memorialists of the time had a good word for her, other than to say that she was very beautiful when she was young.

[3] Charles Gerard, first Baron Gerard of Brandon (ca. 1618–1694) had fought bravely for Charles I in the civil wars.

away, also profiting from his opportunity, according to some people.

Her husband[4] was never willing to enjoy in peace the ten thousand pounds a year that the King offered him in recompense for his dishonour, but abandoned his wife and left the country, and went everywhere making his shame public by too much zeal in justifying himself. The King has been greatly displeased by this, for it made his affair with this woman more scandalous, and in England scandals of this sort are able to produce very evil consequences; the more so because among the Presbyterians there was no lack of men who have made the people and the ignorant lower classes fix their gaze on a king abandoning himself to such open and shameless adultery, and have brought them to consider him as an abyss into which are poured those riches that the people bear so great a burden to contribute for the safety and security of the realm. And to tell the truth, the prodigious amount of money dissipated by this woman, who has no moderation or limit in her desires, passes all bounds and exceeds all belief.[5] She has obtained everything she has asked for and spent all she has obtained, or rather not spent it but squandered it and let it be taken, by whom she knows not; maintaining innumerable relations, friends, servants, domestics, men, women, and children of every sort and kind. With all this she has always been in extreme want of money, so unexampled has been her bad administration and her lavish prodigality. The King's affection has not so much changed her habits that she has denied herself liberties as the fancy took her. With more than one man, they say; but about Harry Jermyn, nephew of the Earl of St. Albans, there seems to be no doubt that he took advantage of the King even at the time when the latter was in the greatest heat of his fervid inclinations.

At first the Queen had some disagreements with her, but realizing that she would only embitter the King, resigned from the contest, admitting her to her presence, together with her children, like the other ladies-in-waiting. There are those who believe that when Madam Castlemaine became a Catholic about four years ago, she wanted only to conciliate the Queen; but I have been assured by one who knows that there were no political ends mixed with this

---

[4] Roger Palmer (1634–1705) married Barbara Villiers in 1659. He was forced to accept the earldom of Castlemaine against his will. He was a man of some ability in languages and mathematics.

[5] Her rapacity has been universally condemned.

resolution of hers, suggested to her only by the fear of death, to which in a dangerous illness she knew she was near. In fact the fear was so pressing and the danger so extreme that the sacraments of our religion were administered to her without sufficient instruction, which was given to her only after her illness. I have indeed learned that at Easter and other solemn feasts, when the Queen appears in public to perform her devotions, and with her all her Catholic court, Madam Castlemaine has had great difficulty in finding confessors who would listen to her confession, there being few of them in England and these few all dependent on the Queen, with whom in this country it is considered very bad to discredit oneself. But this year I am certain that she took communion, for I saw her with my own eyes doing it, together with Bernadino Guasconi. They were the last two who came to communion on Easter morning in the church of St. James under the eyes of the Queen. It has been told to me as certain that a Jesuit had given her absolution.

At the present time this lady is not very beautiful, although she shows the vestiges of a marvellous beauty. She could not possibly carry herself in a worse way than she does; this is, in truth, a defect common to all the English ladies, who, as if they moved by some internal power only from the waist up, trail their thighs and legs behind them in a ridiculous way. However, in her this is an advantage, for not only in her carriage, but in every gesture of the arms and the hands, in every expression of her face, in every glance, in every movement of her mouth, in every word, one recognizes shamelessness and whoredom. At times she gives way to terrible rages. Her jealousy of the reinstatement of the Duchess of Richmond,[6] with whom, in spite of every appearance of irritation in the past, she has always believed the King to be deeply smitten, poisoned her mind with such mortal rancour that in these rages she often shut herself in her apartments, refusing to dine with the King. This obliged him to dine by himself or at the Duchess of Monmouth's, which he has done continually for the last four months.

The custom is like this: a table is set with only one place, for the King, but many more covers stand on the sideboard, which are

---

[6] Frances Teresa Stuart (ca. 1648–1702), one of the greatest beauties at the court, and one of the very few who rejected the attentions of the King, who fell madly in love with her. In 1667 she eloped with the Duke of Richmond, and with her husband was banished from the court, but she was allowed back after a few months.

brought one at a time as the King calls the people with whom he wishes to dine. The regular guests are the Duke, when he is in England, the Duchess of Monmouth, and Lady Castlemaine. Then the others are ladies and gentlemen as it pleases the King to summon them. Among the ladies the Duchess of Buckingham goes there very frequently; among the men Prince Rupert, the Duke of Buckingham, Lord Gerard, Ruvigny, Flammarens, and others of the court as it may happen. There the King relaxes, he is wholly intent on eating; above all he no more remembers that he has a kingdom than would the most private gentlemen who might sit at that table.

The visits to Lady Castlemaine were made regularly twice a day when I was in London. The King was bored with them to the highest degree, but nevertheless went on with them, partly from a sense of obligation and partly because of his good and agreeable nature, which cannot throw off the yoke that another person dares to put upon him. I really believe that the great row that the pious Presbyterian rabble was making throughout the kingdom about this scandal influenced him somewhat, and not less because of this than because of the cooling of his lust for this woman, he renounced, some time ago, certain more public demonstrations, such as being always seen with her in his carriage during his drive in Hyde Park, and in his box at the play.

For a time people were also saying that he was thinking of buying her a mansion with a vast garden near St. James's palace, and thus communicating with Whitehall by way of the park. But when, as I was told, he had considered how much talk such a purchase would have caused at a time when the realm was bleeding from the wounds, still fresh, of so many heavy taxes, and when he was urging Parliament to impose new ones, it seems that his intention cooled off. The evening before my departure a well-informed person said to me, "You will soon hear of the expulsion of our whores, for the King has resolved to be free of them anyhow." "What?" I remarked, "then the King has been to confession?" "No," was the reply, "he wants to behave worse than ever, but as all men of honour do it, secretly, and without keeping the whore beside the throne."

What has happened since then I do not know. I have indeed heard of the reconciliation with the Duchess of Richmond and the frequent visits that the King goes on making to her every day. Some people say that she serves as a pretext, and that in reality all his present inclination is towards Miss Stuart, her sister. It could be anything, but when I reflect on the old passion that the King felt for the Duchess when she was at court as a girl, simply a maid-of-honour; his rages at her clandestine marriage; Castlemaine's jealousy, which might indeed be thought well founded; the cabal of the Earl of Bristol to bring her back into the King's favour, after having gained both his and the husband's confidence by assiduous service and intimacy; and finally above everything else her angelic and wonderful beauty, not at all spoiled by the small-pox, and the mediocrity of that of her sister; all these make this supposition quite unconvincing to me. Many would have it that this is a result of his firm and scrupulous proposal to withdraw entirely and not to stumble once more into a second adultery. The first thing is, whether his scruples are religious or political. If they are political, the remedy is at hand in the tolerance and the presence of the Duke,[7] which are enough to take away from seditious people the means of insinuating a scandal. I am sure that from this tolerance the King could almost promise himself his desires, considering the husband's extreme weakness and the very disastrous state of his fortune, incapable of keeping up his prodigality for long, after having sustained that of his uncle. But if the King's scruples are all reduced to being merely religious, I come back to saying that anything could happen, but I do not think I wrong the King if I do not credit him with as much virtue as a man, made of flesh and blood like others, would need in order to keep this religious resolution steady, firm, and constant under daily temptation.

The current opinion of the Duchess has always been of her extreme virtue and prudence with private gentlemen; with the King, people were talking in a different way. After her marriage, and up to the time of my stay in England, there was not even a shadow of suspicion; indeed both she and her husband were in complete disgrace, and although she was permitted to come to court a month before my departure, his exile continued without remission. During the time that she remained at court, it is known that the King fell madly in love with her and that he used to pass many hours a day alone with her in her apartments. This was enough to make some people speak rashly against her honesty, adding the motive given them by the infinite and extreme distress with which she bore her disgrace and dismissal from the palace. But I am much more strongly persuaded by the social standing of

---

[7] The Duke of Richmond.

the people who have assured me of the contrary, to the advantage of her prudence, as far as one can be assured in such hidden and secret matters.

Then the King has some other temporary attachments of which no account can be given, as they alter continually without coming to the attention of the court. Only two of these can be reported; one concerns Bab May,[8] the other Chiffinch.[9] The former is the Keeper of the Privy Purse and first Assistant at the Close-Stool, an office of the greatest confidence that can be filled by any private gentleman. This man is good natured, of honourable principles, entirely without malice, and full of discretion; It is said that he now occupies the post of Lord Fitzhardinge,[10] who died in the first battle against the Dutch, in the graces of the Countess of Suffolk,[11] one of the Howard family, a lady now of forty years and more, and first Lady of the Bedchamber to the queen. Chiffinch is simply a man-servant, of very ordinary condition, but an old and devoted servant of the King, indeed perhaps the only one who loves him and not the crown. This fellow has a gaming-house in St. James's park where smuggling goes on all the time, to which nobody is admitted except these two men and the merchandise that is continually trafficked in.

They say that among the lower classes the King rarely mixes with women other than girls, of which I think I have some evidence. About three months ago an English actress[12] was in vogue, not of extraordinary beauty but a very graceful dancer. The King came to desire her and made her a gift of a thousand pounds in advance, and another of a diamond ring. Finally she was

---

[8] Baptist May (1629–1698) owed his position to Lady Castlemaine.

[9] William Chiffinch (ca. 1602–1688). After 1666 he was Keeper of the King's Closet, and as such "he was employed by Charles in his most secret business, whether amorous or political." (Anthony Hamilton, *Memoirs of the Comte de Gramont,* tr. Peter Quennell, [London, 1930], p. 337.)

[10] Charles Berkeley (d. 1665), Viscount Fitzharding and Earl of Falmouth, was killed in a naval battle against the Dutch. Burnet thought very highly of him. See *A Supplement to Burnet's History of My Own Time,* etc., ed. H. C. Foxcroft (Oxford, 1902), p. 65.

[11] Barbara Howard, Countess of Suffolk, was first Lady of the Bedchamber to the Queen-Mother.

[12] The two best-known mistresses from the stage are Nell (i.e. Eleanor) Gwyn and Mary Davis. Assuming that "three months ago" refers to the winter of 1667–1668, both might be said to be "in vogue." However, it seems to be established that Nell Gwyn had at least two lovers before becoming the mistress of Charles II: Charles Hart, an actor, and Charles, Lord Buckhurst. The wits said that the King was her "Charles III."

brought to him, but when he wanted to embrace her she threw herself, very frightened, at his feet and declared, weeping, that she was not a virgin. The King wanted to know who had deflowered her and, learning that it had been the Duke of Monmouth, went away disturbed and never sought her again. However, the court believed that the King had had knowledge of her, and many would have it that the intrigue still persisted, but I think I can say that the truth is as I have said.

For certain merely convivial parties the King at times has used a house of Lord Arlington's, outside St. James's park; but I have never heard that he has taken women there, but simply some gentlemen whom he has wanted to treat with great friendliness. He did this two years ago to the Spanish ambassador, who drank bravely like all the others, and I know from someone who happened towards daybreak to see them returning to Whitehall after dinner, that the King and the ambassador and a handful of others, having thrown away their wigs, came along leaping and dancing in the moonlight, preceded by the whole band of violins, in imitation of King David before the ark, and in the street:

Chi gettò'l vino per diversi spilli,
e chi arrivò facendo billi billi.[13]

Before leaving the subject of the King I have to speak of a certain English lackey called Booten. This fellow caused me terrible suspicions about what his trade might be. He is a page, sixteen years old, handsome, clean-shaven, witty, impertinent, and furnished with certain parts more suitable to a giant than a boy. He has access to the King's bedroom at all hours, talks familiarly with him, and in fact the whole situation looks bad. I was finally assured that his first introduction was by the liveliness of his ready wit and his comical and pleasing chatter. He now gives even more delight by recounting all the adventures that the special virtue of his great parts leads him into with the London ladies, in whose houses and at whose tables the King's favour makes him welcomed and received like any gentleman. Between this and the requests for money that he continually makes at court, he succeeds in putting together a considerable quantity of gold pieces. Since this suspicion of mine has disappeared, not only have I failed to observe anything else that would raise any others of this kind, but I have had indubitable

---

[13] Alessandro Tassoni, *La secchia rapita*, 8, 61. I shall not attempt a translation.

proofs of the virginal purity of the King and the Duke in any kind of concupiscence except the natural one.

About the Duchess of York[14] much might be said, even about the former times when she was in the service of the Princess Royal. There is still an opinion that the Duke was not the first to have knowledge of her. I have had no information about things nowadays forgotten. The newest gossip is about her close friendship with Sir Henry Sidney,[15] a very handsome and graceful young man in the service of the Duke, who on his return from the battle against the Dutch thought that he had better dismiss him from his service and send him home. The death of Lady Denham,[16] which followed soon afterwards, gave rise to other talk about the Duchess having her poisoned in revenge for the expulsion of Sidney, and this winter it is suspected that Parliament, under the liberty of free speech requested of the King, might want to make inquiries about this, out of their hatred of the family of the Chancellor. But I do not find that this poison business is acknowledged by sensible men as being beyond doubt, the more so as there is a shrewd opinion that calls into question whether the familiarity between the Duke and the lady passed beyond wooing and gallantry. But in this case I am more inclined to believe in something more. To repeat all the chatter, there are also those who say that the Duke, as a second revenge for the death of the lady, caught the pox on purpose to communicate it to his wife. But she has now become less jealous of her husband and it appears that they have agreed to live in peace without disturbing each other. In fact the duke cheerfully diverted himself with Miss Churchill,[17] and when she left a new affair with Miss Libonard[18] began to appear. Both were very beautiful, and were maids-of-honour of the Duchess.

The Duchess, on the other hand, knowing that she cannot have everything to her liking, satisfies herself with the unrestricted supervision—recently obtained—of all the Duke's household and

---

[14] See note 32, p. 37.

[15] Henry Sidney (1641–1704) had been Master of the Horse to the Duchess of York. He was accounted the handsomest man in England. Pepys reports this scandalous tale on November 16, 1665.

[16] Margaret Brooke (ca. 1646–1667), who married Sir John Denham in 1665, was acknowledged by the Duke of York as his mistress during the following year. Her death of a painful illness in January, 1667 gave rise to the rumours reported by Magalotti. It is accepted that she died from natural causes.

[17] Arabella Churchill (1648–1730), eldest daughter of Sir Winston Churchill, had several children by the Duke of York.

[18] I have been unable to identify this lady.

the administration of all his business, and we have to believe, for evil people say so, that the close intimacy that she has with the Marquis de Blanquefort,[19] Captain of the Duke's guard, is all concerned with good economic direction, as one who holds the private purse of the his lord.

Of the Queen-Mother nothing can be said except that she is at present full of the most tender devotion and of indiscretion. Her past life is very well known, as are the arts with which, when she had come to have absolute domination over the poor King, her husband, adhering to the opinions of France, she imbued him with principles so pernicious to his real interests, as his unhappy end showed. When she saw that he was so firmly held by his love for her she treated him with unheard-of strictness; I have been assured on good authority that he often had to buy his pleasures with money.[20] Equally well-known is her long affair with the Earl of St. Albans,[21] who, after the reform of his morals, became her spiritual husband. With all this the Earl does not omit to procure himself other relief; he is having an affair with a woman whom he keeps, having had her married to a major-domo of his, named Vorcel. Of this woman he has two fine little boys, eleven and twelve years old, whom he retains in his service as pages. It was a revolting thing to see the King and his brothers having to beg their bread while they were in France, and at the very time when subscriptions were being held at the court to maintain them, to hear of them losing a thousand or fifteen hundred doubloons in an evening to the Earl of St. Albans.

Prince Rupert served his apprenticeship in his youth. He has not given up amusing himself, but he does not want his pleasures to cost him much money or much diligence. Therefore he likes to get it over with and to spend little, so that all sorts of people suit him. His most highly placed affairs, which he had ten months ago, were with one Miss Bard,[22] whom I have not seen, and a Mrs. Cecil[23] (married, if I am not mistaken, to the son of the Earl of

---

[19] Louis Duras, Marquis of Blancfort in the French peerage (ca. 1640–1709), later Earl of Feversham, having been naturalized in England in 1665.

[20] This is one of the items of hearsay in which our author occasionally indulges. The slander has been very persistent.

[21] See note 79, p. 59.

[22] Frances Bard, daughter of Viscount Bellamont. Prince Rupert had a son by her (Crinò).

[23] This was the wife of James Cecil, who succeeded to the earldom of Salisbury in 1669.

Salisbury), whose greatest beauty lies in her figure and in the whiteness of her skin. An amusing incident is told of her. She was at the theatre with the prince in a box that had only balusters in front of it, and he, throwing a cloak over them like a tablecloth, thought he could safely use his hands under the lady's clothes; but as the cornice, projecting forward, held the cloak quite away from the balusters, the progress of this fine and gallant operation could easily be observed by a group of gentlemen of the court.

Whoever wanted to recount all the dissipations of the Duke of Monmouth[24] would have to make too long a search. It is enough to know about him that he and the Duke of Richmond have been the two most intrepid patrons of bawdy-houses in London. The Duke has sweated five or six times to cure himself of the pox in the bones, of which it is no wonder that he has reaped such a good harvest, as he has never refused a place to whatever rabble his lackeys have put into his hands, without disdaining to dip in where many had dipped before and would do so after him. Indeed, his greatest pleasure has been to see them operate in his presence and to drink in their company in the middle of the entertainment. I have been told that when that bastard of the Duke of Bellegarde's, by whom he had been educated in France, came to England last year, he brought one of his whores with him, with whom the Duke fell in love. Not having been able to forget his desire for her, for no other motive than his whim he went to France with Lord Russell,[25] son of the Earl of Bedford, and finally succeeded in defeating the modesty of this woman. I hear later that she has written very great abuse of him in England, but I have not been able to understand the circumstances; indeed, with what little knowledge I have of the habits of the Duke, I imagine that it all comes of his not having paid her. He played the same trick on one Miss Greers, a woman of good condition who was stolen from her father's house by the Duke of Richmond and held for several days in a country house under promise of marriage. It is true that when she realized how simple she had been she escaped from him and, not daring to go back to her father, took shelter in the house of a doctor called the Cavalier de Vaux.[26] This man is the son of a French father, but living in England; he has travelled in Italy, and

---

[24] See note 37, p. 40.
[25] William Russell (1639–1683).
[26] This is almost certainly Sir Theodore de Vaux, F.R.S. (1628–1694), one of the royal physicians.

for all his privilege as a doctor I think he knows very little medicine. He is an intimate protégé of Henry Howard of Norfolk,[27] and I believe that he serves to treat the sufferings of the mind rather than the infirmities of the body. I am also given to understand that this young refugee of his largely earned his living for him. He let me see her and talk with her; but when I heard from another friend about a little matter of twenty doubloons, the conversation was suddenly broken off. Now the Duke of Monmouth promised her a hundred pounds, and when he had what he wanted of her, gave her nothing. This winter he happened to be in Paris at the same time as Count Vaudemont, a bastard of the Duke of Lorraine; also a well-made young man. The decision of the ladies was that Monmouth was more charming to look at and Vaudemont more enjoyable. And I really believe that they are well-informed, because in some parts of his body Monmouth is in a wretched and pitiable state. His great confidant is a certain knight, Verne, a person of very ordinary birth, but who passes for a gentleman, not less because he has the Order of the Bath than because of an estate that yields seven or eight thousand pounds a year. He is such a horrid pale fellow, effeminate and hairless, that at first sight, he looks like a very fine bedspread for a woman. His friendship with the Duke has brought him into great favour with the Duchess, and this gives rise to gossip, especially to the belief that Verne is paying out money to give the Duke the opportunity of getting out of some amour. I do not know what the truth is, nor am I resolved to believe all that has been told me in this matter on the word of the people who gave me the report.

The opinion about Lord Arlington is that he has a secret intimacy with Madam Scroop,[28] a lady in the Queen's circle, following the Abbé d'Aubigny,[29] according to what they say. The latter is the Grand Almoner, and I have learned to my great amazement that, apart from his pleasures with women, he also went in for amusing himself with young men, for in this matter he was closely associated with the Duke of Buckingham. This opinion is so contrary to the idea that I had about the virtue of this worthy ecclesiastic that I could not adopt it and keep my esteem and veneration of him; so I am forcing my intellect not to lend credence

---

[27] See also p. 114 below.
[28] Mary Scroop (Crinò).
[29] Louis Stuart, known as the Abbé d'Aubigny (1619–1665).

to such iniquitous reports, which I declare that I write about as excesses of calumny, not as pictures of the truth.

Such are the intrigues of the chief nobles of the court. Now to begin to give details of the tricks and private amours of all the maids-of-honour and the ladies who frequent the court would be an endless task. First, I confess that I do not know about all of them, and I have forgotten many that I have been told about, such as things that consist only of two names—so-and-so with so-and-so, and nothing else—without adducing any consequence or having any connection with the interests of real people.

It seems to me that I can establish a principle without wronging anyone whatsoever: among the ladies of the court and of London, there is little honesty. In the rest of the realm they tell me that there is more innocence; but in the dominant city moderation in women passes for poorness of spirit and not for virtue. However, they love nobleman, because they are proud, and neat and well-made men, because they do it for their own pleasure, apart from those who are driven by necessity, and these are universally infected. Therefore in England we have the reverse of the proverb which says "He who does not pay the whore pays the doctor." Some of these women like lackeys, but woe to them if this ever comes to be known, for they at once lose credit and reputation, not less among women than among men.

The Bodyguard of the King, the Duke, and the General

Of old the kings of England have had only two corps of guards, one called the Yeomen of the Guard, the other the Gentlemen Pensioners. By an Act of Parliament of 1660 passed at the restoration of the present King there have now been added the horse guards, armed with breastplate and back plate, steel cap, sword, pistol, and carbine; and it was proclaimed that the corps should consist of 600 men. It is divided into three companies of 200 men each, the first called the King's guards, the second the Duke's, and the third the General's.

Officers of the King's Company of Guards

Captain: Lord Gerard.[30] this man is esteemed one of the best soldiers in England; he had his training in the kingdom at the time of the civil wars, in which he was a lieutenant of cavalry, and once in an engagement he fought against Cromwell, whose troops he defeated in spite of the enemy's superiority in numbers. Later he had campaigned in the service of the Dutch, and after the exile of the King fought in some other campaign in Flanders, serving the Spanish as a volunteer. At this time he was made a lord. In his commission as Captain of the guards the King makes very meticulous mention of his services, and especially of the many wounds he received in rendering them, as is testified by his whole body, covered with scars. He was born with a very small fortune, although of a family not at all obscure.[31] As a young man he was always fighting; he was loved by the women, and it is said that a lady of high rank died of despair and jealousy for him. He always looks to his own interest, and his soldiers know it. He abhors wine,

---

[30] See note 3, p. 71. Concerning the officers of these regiments, see Charles Dalton, *English Army Lists and Commission Registers* (London, 1892).

[31] Not for at least three generations, since his great grandfather, Sir Gilbert Gerard (d. 1593) became a prominent legal light at the court of Elizabeth I.

and his age now makes him care little for the pleasures of the senses. His chief amusement is horse-racing and the huge bets made on such occasions, according to the English custom. A great many people turned against him this winter because of an appeal made to Parliament by a gentleman from whom he had taken an estate with an income of 600 pounds. The plaintiff claimed that he had obtained the judgment in devious ways, by corruption and false witnesses, but when I left the court it seemed that things were taking a better turn for him and that the accusation was not going to subsist.

Lieutenants: Sir Gilbert Gerard, Major-General Egerton,[32] Sir Thomas Sandys. Both the other companies of guards have only two lieutenants; although this one has three, when one dies the commission will not be given to anyone, as it is desired to make it the same as the others.

The first of these lieutenants is a first cousin of the Captain and has been a colonel in the King's army. The second originally served against the King as major-general under Cromwell, and later returned to the King's side and contributed to his restoration as much as anyone else. The third was a colonel of infantry in France, deemed the most handsome young man of his time, so that all the women went mad for love of him. He fought on horseback with pistols and then with a sword, in a duel of two against two, of which he was the only survivor, covered with wounds, leaving all the other three dead on the field, for which exploit Cardinal Mazarin gave him a pension of 1000 crowns, which was paid him as long as he served France. It is quite true that all his merits come down to handsomeness of body and ferocity of spirit, without his mind matching such fine properties with any gifts.

Ensign: Mr. Stanley,[33] son of the Earl of Derby whose head was cut off, together with that of the Duke of Hamilton,[34] after the death of the late King, by order of Parliament. He is a young man of twenty-five who has been in various actions at sea.

Besides these officers, every company of guards has a quartermaster and eight corporals.

---

[32] Randolph Egerton (d. 1681) had served as Major-General to Charles I. Miss Crinò identifies Egerton with a member of the Parliament that was sitting in 1669.

[33] Edward Stanley, one of the four sons of James Stanley, seventh Earl of Derby (1607–1651).

[34] James, first Duke of Hamilton (1606–1649).

Pay:[35] The captain has forty-four shillings a day and if he wishes, at least forty deadheads,[36] between which, and many other things, his office yields from five to six thousand pounds a year. The lieutenant has twenty-two shillings a day, without too many other things to avail himself of; the ensign has sixteen, the quartermaster twelve, the corporals eight, and the ordinary soldiers four. All the officers and soldiers of the other two companies have the same pay.

Officers of the Duke's Company of Guards

Captain: the Marquis of Blanchefort,[37] a Frenchman of the Duras family, nephew of Marshal Turenne. He is a younger son of his house. As a young man he learned his trade in Flanders, first under his uncle and then in the service of the Spaniards, in company with the Duke, his patron, who from that time began to like him until, growing in favour day by day, he has now risen to occupy the first place in his good graces, and in those of the Duchess. He was Lieutenant of his company when its Captain, Lord Fitzharding,[38] Earl of Falmouth, was killed in the first naval battle against the Dutch. The Duke was at this engagement. With other honest emoluments, he has those six or seven thousand pounds a year like the other captains of the guard. Huguenot as he was, he has embraced the Anglican church, becoming a naturalized Englishman. He is the Keeper of the Duke's Privy Purse, a young and handsome cavalier, wise, sober, and discreet, and generally liked by the court and everyone else. With his soldiers he is just and liberal, and has made the greatest effort to conquer the natural repugnance of the English to being commanded by foreigners and especially by Frenchmen. He has succeeded very well in this, and is most happy about it.

Lieutenants: Colonel Worden, Major Dutton. Both of these are very good and expert soldiers, inasmuch as they were trained in the civil wars.

Ensign: Sir Sidney Godolphin. This man was ensign of the Duke's bodyguard in Flanders, when he was Lieutenant-General

---

[35] Regarding the pay of officers, both military and naval, the scales were much more diverse than our author supposed. Cf. Clifford Walton, *History of the British Standing Army, A.D. 1660 to 1700* (London, 1894), chap. 29.

[36] "Deadheads," that is to say soldiers who are on the payroll but do not exist. The Italian term is *piazze morte*.

[37] See note 19, p. 79.

[38] See note 10, p. 76.

for the Spanish. Here he learned soldiering and saved the Duke's life at the battle of Dunkirk by killing with a pistol shot an Englishman who had reached the duke's side and was about to seize him in order to kill him.

Officers of the General's Company of Guards

Captain: Sir Philip Howard, brother of the Earl of Carlisle, who was the King's ambassador in Denmark. He is the second son of his house, from which he gets a large allowance. He has always been captain of the General's company of guards, even before the restoration of the King. As a young man he travelled a great deal, but he learned the art of war only in the revolutions of the kingdom. In the last war against the Dutch he was in all the three naval battles, although he could have got out of the first one because the General was not there. He is a man who will have the goodwill of other men and who is extraordinarily fond of women.

Lieutenants: Mr. Monk, Mr. Collingwood. The first is the General's cousin and has always served under him since the recent war; the second is still very young.

Ensign: Mr. Watson, a cavalier of very fine appearance, accomplished and deserving, and a favourite protégé of the general's.

After the peace of Breda the King reduced each of these companies to half strength, so that at present there are only one hundred men in each one. But it is believed that this reform is not going to be continued and that any small disturbance among the lower classes will persuade him of the expediency and necessity of restoring them to their original number. He cannot meet with any difficulty in this, because this number was fixed by Parliament. It is true that if it becomes intolerable to keep Parliament sitting, there is a great risk that the reform may fail over the question of pay for the officers and soldiers, if the House of Commons does not once more provide the funds especially for this.

These three companies have nothing to do with the rest of the military, and in time of war they march in the most honourable place of all the army. I have also been told (it is true that I have not had any proof) that the three captains of the guards, under the General, are higher in command than all the colonels of infantry and cavalry.

All three of these companies have quarters in London and every day they mount a squadron of fifty men, who always follow the coaches of the King, the Queen, and the Duke, and when the

King goes by water, only six of them go in a special boat, and then they take off their riding boots and carry carbines on their shoulders. When he goes in his coach he has twenty-five, the Queen and the Duke twelve each. When the King and the Duke mount their horses for hunting or to ride in the country they are followed by the same number—each one of them respectively—as when they go in their coaches. Besides this the King has a trumpeter in front of the officer who marches at the head of the guard, which the Queen and the Duke do not have.

The Yeomen of the Guard

These are a very ancient guard,[39] a hundred in number. They wear cloaks of bright scarlet with strips of black velvet in front; in the middle of the chest and behind the shoulders they have the crowned rose, and on this side and that the King's monogram in gold embroidery. Usually the tallest and biggest men in the kingdom are chosen, and their function is to help the guards in the anteroom and at public ceremonies, like the emperor's guards elsewhere, to prevent a crush of people. When the bodyguard were not there they used to follow the King's coach on foot, with halberds on their shoulders, but now they remain in the hall, where they eat or smoke or read the Scriptures. They are paid fifty pounds a year each, and as much roast beef as they want on the days when they stand on guard. Therefore they are known in mockery by the name "beefeaters."[40] Their captain is Lord Grandison,[41] of the family of the Duke of Buckingham and a close relation. I could find out nothing about his social standing except that he is the uncle of Lady Castlemaine; I do not know how much he is paid.

The Pensioners' Guard

This is also a very ancient establishment of guards, going back to the times of the first kings of England.[42] It consists of a

---

[39] This famous guard, often confused in the public mind with the warders of the Tower of London, was formed in 1485 by Henry VII. See H. Brackenbury, *The History of His Majesty's Body Guard*, etc. (London, 1905), p. 29.

[40] The origin of the epithet "beefeater" has been a subject of dispute. Walton, *History*, p. 9, has it that the word is "merely an anglicised corruption of the word "buffetiers," that is, cupbearers or side-board-waiters." See also Sir R. Hennell, *The History of the King's Bodyguard of the Yeomen of the Guard* (London, 1904), pp. 28–29, who dismisses this idea out of hand.

[41] George Villiers, fourth Viscount Grandison (d. 1699).

[42] Magalotti was misinformed, for this guard was established by Henry

company of one hundred gentlemen, each paid a hundred pounds a
year, who do nothing but attend public functions in their black or
coloured attire, with small gilded halberds in their hands, making
a cordon in front of the throne of the King when he receives
ambassadors or accompanying him when he goes in public on
Sundays or feast days from his apartments to the chapel. Their
captain is Baron Belasyse,[43] a very old man who fifty years ago was
considered by everyone the handsomest young man of his time. He
was the Governor of Tangiers, from which he returned two years
ago with a nestegg reckoned at twenty thousand pounds. This
office is a very profitable one, so that the King is disinclined to let
the governors take root there. Lord Belasyse is very civil and
affable. He was a colonel in England and demonstrated his great
courage on every occasion.

VIII in 1509, the year of his accession. See Brackenbury, *His Majesty's Body
Guard,* p. 32.

[43] John, Baron Belasyse (1614–1689) had fought for Charles I in the civil
wars. As he was only fifty-four when Magalotti saw him, his appearance fifty
years earlier can scarcely have been as described. His leaving the governorship of
Tangier in 1666 was due to his being unable, as a Catholic, to take the oath of
conformity.

Standing Regiments[44]

There are five regiments kept mobilized by the King of England: one of cavalry and four of infantry. The cavalry regiment always remains quartered in the country, is called the King's regiment, and is composed of eight companies. The Colonel is the Earl of Oxford,[45] second Earl of England. He is of the De Vere family, if not the first, then certainly the second of the whole kingdom. He was born a younger son and is now the first, indeed the only one of his house, for not only has he no children but he is not even married,[46] although he is forty. At first he served the Dutch against Spain, and then the Spanish against France in Flanders, and finally he became expert through long experience in the civil wars of the realm. He is a poor gentleman, not having a patrimony of more than three or four thousand pounds, and with this a heavy debt although this is to many people in small sums. Nevertheless he is splendid and liberal, and they say that apart from his provisions he draws no profit from his regiment, but generously distributes what remains among his officers.

Pay of Officers and Soldiers of the Cavalry Regiment

The colonel has forty shillings a day, the lieutenant-colonel. . . . ,[47] the captain sixteen, which between one thing and another makes the office worth a thousand pounds a year, clear. The captains' lieutenants, twelve shillings, which go up to twenty, for these men are not like the lieutenants of the guards, of which the captains all have such a great place at court that they

---

[44] Again Magalotti simplifies the actual situation. See Walton, *History*. For the violent opposition to the keeping of standing armies, see Lois G. Schwoerer, *"No Standing Armies": The Anti-Army Ideology in Seventeenth-Century England* (Baltimore, 1974).

[45] Aubrey de Vere (1626–1703), twentieth Earl of Oxford. He was really the eldest son of the nineteenth earl.

[46] In fact he married twice, and by the second wife he had a son and three daughters.

[47] A lacuna in the MS.

appropriate all the emoluments to themselves. Ensigns, ten shillings, which also go up to fourteen. The quartermasters, who correspond to *maréchaux de logis* in France, eight shillings; nevertheless they find ways of rendering their office more lucrative than that of the lieutenants.

[*The Infantry Regiments*]

The infantry paid by the King consists of only four regiments. The first, called the King's regiment, has 2400 men, divided into twenty-four companies. Half of these stay in the country and half in London. Colonel Russell,[48] brother of the very wealthy Earl of Bedford; a man of fifty, younger son of his house, has twenty shillings a day. Lieutenant-Colonel Grey,[49] the oldest colonel in England, gets fifteen; he is getting very old and has served in Holland and in England; of quite a good family. Major Rollstone,[50] gets twelve shillings a day. First Captain Sir Thomas Daniel, a gentleman of good family, an old and esteemed soldier, commands the King's company, that is to say the one that raises the royal standard. His pay, like that of all the other captains, is eight shillings a day, which in any case comes to those 500 pounds a year. Lieutenants, four shillings, and they make it six.[51] Ensigns, three shillings, and they make it five. Soldiers, tenpence, which is the ordinary pay of all the soldiers in the land. The King's regiment has red jackets over dark blue, the livery of the King.

Second, the regiment of the Duke of York, otherwise called the admiralty regiment, is composed of fourteen companies with a hundred men in each. Colonel, Sir Chichester Wrey,[52] an old soldier of good family. This regiment serves maritime requirements, and is always quartered at the ports and in other coastal localities. Its task is to visit the ships, and when the fleet is mobilized the regiment is distributed among the vessels, and the same number are recruited to replace on land those who embark. Meanwhile these are directed and trained in several companies from those twenty which are under the discipline of other officers who always remain on land. They have yellow jackets lined with the livery of the Duke.

---

[48] Colonel John Russell (d. 1687).
[49] This may be Colonel Edward Grey.
[50] Probably William Rolleston.
[51] There was an elaborate scheme of pay and allowances. See Walton, *History*.
[52] Sir Chichester Wrey, Bart., of Trebitch, Cornwall (d. 1668).

Third, the General's regiment; it always stays in London, lodged near Holborn. Colonel: Miller,[53] an old soldier, an ancient follower and intimate creature of the General's. This regiment also is formed of fourteen companies of a hundred men each, as are regularly all the regiments in England. Red jackets, lined with green.

Fourth, the Holland regiment; Colonel: Sydney,[54] an old and esteemed soldier of very good family. This regiment was in Holland for many years, paid by the States-General, but since the late war the King has brought it back to England, after letting it train in the science of arms at the expense of his enemies. Red jackets, lined with yellow.

The King's regiment has a red standard, the Duke's yellow, the General's green, and Sydney's red and white. To these may be added the Scottish regiment, otherwise called the Queen's, commanded by the Márquis of Douglas.[55] The officers and soldiers are all Scottish. For a long time this regiment has served in Flanders whenever there was no war in England; otherwise it crosses the sea and receives pay from its King, like the other regiments.

I have spoken of Douglas on other occasions, but I will only add that as a boy he was a page of the King of France and had obtained the regiment when he was twenty, after the death of his uncle. Thus he was brought up to favour the French. When this regiment came over to England on the declaration of war on this crown by France, it was few in number and badly equipped. But last year it returned to France with 1500 soldiers, all in the very best order.

All this soldiery is very well paid, the infantry weekly, the cavalry every month, and the guards every two months. Every day four companies of infantry stand guard over the royal houses, two from the King's regiment and two from the General's, and these are distributed at Whitehall palace, and in the park and at the palace of St. James, the usual abode of the Duke in summer. In the same way another company goes every day to guard the Tower of London. However, none are usually quartered in the city except the General's regiment and half that of the King, apart from the bodyguards, as I said before.

---

[53] John Miller. He had been in Monk's guard in 1660. He seems to have been a major, not a colonel (Dalton, *Army Lists*).

[54] Robert Sydney (d. 1668), third son of Robert, Earl of Leicester.

[55] Lord George Douglas (ca. 1636–1692), later Earl of Dumbarton.

[*The Ordinary Militia*]

Besides the above-mentioned regiments there are the ordinary militia, which are said to amount to 100,000 effectives, of which the City of London alone furnishes 40,000. They have all the officers I have described, under which each company drills, and on occasion they take up their arms at the sound of a drum. The Earl of Craven[56] is the General of this militia. He is a man whose reputation was won in the German war, as rich as any other lord in England, a close friend of Monk, and who after the death of the Elector Palatine was the putative husband of the Queen of Bohemia.[57] In this number of 100,000 are included 20,000 horse, furnished by the nobles, who regularly send one of their servants on horseback to all the parades, with a pair of pistols at the saddle-bow and a leather jerkin on the back, to be trained. They say that they sometimes do not turn out much inferior to other soldiery, thanks to the continual drill, the ferocity of the nation, and the liberty that they must always defend, when it happens that they have to take up arms against an external enemy.

However, General Monk commands all the three regiments of the land forces and his pay is ten pounds sterling a day.

---

[56] William Craven (1606–1697). It was rumoured that he had secretly married Elizabeth, sister of Charles I, after the death of her husband, the Elector Palatine, but there is no real evidence for this.

[57] Elizabeth, sister of Charles I, who married the Elector Palatine shortly before he was driven from his Kingdom of Bohemia. She was doubly unfortunate in that the Parliament during the interregnum refused to pay the pension she had been promised.

The Naval Forces[58]

The royal fleet of England is composed of three squadrons. The first flies the red flag (which is the colour of England) with the red cross in a small white field quartered in a corner of the flag, and the admiral also flies the standard of the realm, embroidered in gold and silver. The second squadron has the flag dark blue, and the third white, each with the same red cross quartered as above. Each squadron has its admiral, vice-admiral, and rear-admiral, so that the fleet is commanded by nine principal officers, called *flag officers* in English, from whom the captains who command the other vessels receive their orders. What the commander-in-chief does the other admirals do, and what the other admirals do every vessel has to do.

The admirals carry the flag at the mainmast, the vice-admirals at the foremast and the rear-admirals at the mizzen mast.

Every vessel of the first rate usually serves as flagship of the squadron, and because it has no other captain than the admiral, it is given four lieutenants, who take up the command at the death of the senior officer, and so on down, according to the seniority of their commissions. No first-rate, when there are more than three, ever goes in a squadron with the others, and it disdains even to go with the vice-admiral. In such an event it therefore goes under the command of a simple captain and four lieutenants, obeying the high-admiral not as a minor officer but as a volunteer. Then if it happens that one of the admirals is taken or defeated or sunk or ordered to return to some English port while the fleet still remains at sea, this captain will take command in his place, until he returns. This occurred in the most recent battle, where the *Royal Sovereign,* which was a volunteer, made up for the lack of the *Royal Charles,* sent back to Harwich for repairs.

---

[58] The great source for the naval history of this period is, of course, the Pepys collection of manuscripts at Magdalen College, Cambridge. A great deal can be learned from the *Descriptive Catalogue of the Naval Manuscripts in the Pepysian Library* compiled by J. R. Tanner, 4 vols. (Naval Records Society, 1903–1923).

The Duke is the High-Admiral. He gets ten pounds a day, which in wartime goes up to forty thousand and more a year; in peacetime he also gets a great deal extra, but not nearly as much as that. In the absence of the Duke the following admirals have acted for him at various times: Prince Rupert, the Duke of Albemarle, the Earl of Sandwich.[59] I am now going to say something about the last, as I have not named him elsewhere. He is of very noble blood, but the younger son of his house. He served the republic and Cromwell as one of the admirals. He was sent by Cromwell to take the silver fleet from the Spaniards. When this retired into the harbour of Teneriffe, defended by good fortifications, he nevertheless went in with his squadron, took part of the fleet and sent nearly all the rest to the bottom. In the war against the Dutch he was an admiral in company with Generals Blake[60] and Monk, and in the battle where Tromp[61] was, the greater part of the victory was ascribed to him. Then he was sent by Cromwell in supreme command of a fleet of thirty ships to the Sound to help the Swedes in the siege of Copenhagen. The Dutch, under the command of Opdam,[62] came to aid the Danes from the other direction, and Sandwich (on orders from Cromwell) let them do all that they wanted, without firing even a single gun, so that the King of Sweden was obliged to retire. At the time of the King's restoration Sandwich was Supreme Commander of the Fleet, and contributed, not less than others, to his service, for which he was rewarded by being made an Earl and Knight of the Garter, and with the title of Lieutenant-Admiral under the Duke. He was also in the first battle of the most recent war, where the Duke of York was in person. But the origin of his misfortunes was the task given him to capture the ships of the Dutch East Indies Company, in which he gave the opportunity for people to believe that he had been corrupted by the Dutch with great riches. What happened was this. He had gone out towards the north to meet their fleet from the Indies, reinforced with more than thirty ships from Smyrna, sent to meet the warships as a very good convoy. Sandwich met them when they were all damaged by a storm, so that he could have taken all of

---

[59] Edward Montagu, first Earl of Sandwich (1625–1672). The poor strategy described by Magalotti has had various explanations.
[60] Robert Blake (1599–1657).
[61] The great Dutch admiral, Maarten Tromp (1597–1653), who died in a naval battle.
[62] Jacob van Opdam (1610–1665).

them. But nevertheless, contented with only those vessels that he could not help taking, he called back with cannon signals all the captains who were going after new prizes. In consequence only two of the Indies fleet (sold in London for 300,000 pounds) were taken, and another sent to the bottom, twenty of those from Smyrna and eight warships; all, so to speak, without firing a shot. Shortly before this he had let Ruyter[63] pass with a little squadron of only ten warships, when he was nearby with his whole fleet and absolute master of the sea. For all these faults he was therefore deprived of his commission as Vice-Admiral and sent in an honourable exile to Spain as ambassador. He is there now, and gets some praise for the part he has played in concluding the peace with Portugal.[64] While I was in London they were saying that he would return towards the end of the present summer.

The Vice-Admiral of the red squadron is Sir Robert Holmes.[65] This is the man who, of all the naval officers who commanded in the recent war, has been most talked of. As a boy he was a page to Prince Rupert, under whom he had his training at sea, remaining with him all the time when he was a freebooter with three or four vessels that had abandoned Cromwell's party and declared in favour of the King. Later it was he who at the beginning of November, 1664 began the war against Holland in Guinea, driving them (as is thought, by order of the King, although the latter later disowned the entire operation) from all their posts on that shore with a small squadron of vessels that he had for cruising in these seas. On this occasion he collected very great riches, for these are the only places from which England gets her gold. Shortly afterwards, when the Dutch had demanded satisfaction for the actions of Holmes, the King, not thinking it a suitable time to break with them, sent him to the Tower; but soon afterwards, when action against Holland was undertaken, he set him at liberty and gave him the command of one of the best ships. In the first battle he sent to the bottom the vessel of the young Tromp,[66] who, his reputation offended, conceived such a great rivalry with him that he challenged him to fight him man to man

---

[63] Michel de Ruyter (1607–1676).

[64] This was the peace of Lisbon, which made Portugal finally independent of Spain.

[65] Sir Robert Holmes (1622–1692). Pepys lists him as Rear-Admiral of the red (Tanner, *Descriptive Catalogue*, 1, 314).

[66] Cornelis van Tromp (1629–1691).

with equal ships at the next battle. While this was going on he was knighted and made a Rear-Admiral by the King and given a ship that had not yet touched the water, called the *Defiance*, mounted with about sixty guns, a number equal to that of his enemy. He met him in the next battle and for the second time sent to the bottom the vessel of Tromp, who saved himself by swimming to another ship. Finally, after the third and last battle, it was he who suggested to the Duke of Albemarle that he should burn the ships at Vlie, reserving for himself the command of a thousand men who were to make a landing, which he did without losing one of them. I had forgotten to add that he is also captain of a company in the General's regiment, and that recently he was one of the seconds who fought in the duel between the Duke of Buckingham and the Earl of Shrewsbury.

The Rear-Admiral of the red is Sir Joseph Jordan,[67] an old soldier of great repute, for in his time there has been scarcely a sea battle at which he has not been.

The Admiral of the blue is Sir Jeremiah Smith.[68] This man made himself famous by saving the ship and the person of the Duke in the first battle of this latest war. He was second-in-command to the Duke, and seeing that the Dutch flagship commanded by Opdam had come with great resolution to attack the Duke, went between them, receiving all the broadsides of the Dutch flagship, which was shooting at long range according to the custom of that nation. That of the Duke, waiting for them, was not yet firing so as to do it at closer range in the English way. Smith received the broadside, which left more than sixty men dead, and among them all his officers. He replied so luckily that he fired the magazine of Opdam's ship, blowing it up. Opdam had already been wounded by a musket shot. However, Smith is a soldier of fortune like all the others, born and bred on the water, so to speak. At present he is very rich, like all the ship captains, because of the gains they make by escorting merchant ships. As a reward for the above-mentioned action he was knighted and made one of the admirals.

You should know that the High-Admiral has two supporting ships and a large number of fireships that follow him closely. For supporting ships they choose vessels manned by the choicest crews and commanded by the bravest captains and the most expert

---

[67] Sir Joseph Jordan (1603–1685). Pepys spells the name Jorden, which seems unlikely.

[68] Sir Jeremiah Smith (d. 1675).

officers of the whole fleet, for in defence of the High-Admiral they always have to run the greatest risks.

The Vice-Admiral of the blue is Sir Edward Spragge,[69] an Irishman, a soldier of fortune but of a very good family. He served in France and when he came back to serve his King, was knighted and made a flag officer. It was he who sank the flagship of Zeeland in the second battle.

The Rear-Admiral of the blue is Captain Kempthorne,[70] a man very famous in the Levant, where he fought various battles against the Turks and always won them, so that in this latest war he has got himself very great praise.

The Admiral of the white is Sir Thomas Allin,[71] a very brave soldier and sailor. It was he who captured the French ship called the *Ruby*, commanded by M. de la Roche, who, seeing the white standard and thinking it was of the French fleet, went and gave himself into his hands. Realizing his error when there was no time to correct it, he defended himself for a long time, with great foolhardiness rather than courage.

The Rear-Admiral of the white is Sir John Harman.[72] This man served Cromwell's republic at one time. In the second battle of this war he distinguished himself by freeing his ship from three fireships, when she had already been set on fire in some places and when his sailors had already jumped into the sea. Then he, alone with his lieutenant, got away from the fireships and they saved themselves. He was knighted for this operation.

Besides the flag officers already mentioned, the following are renowned above the other naval men:

Sir William Penn.[73] At the time of the republic he was Cromwell's Lieutenant-General in Ireland and later served him (for he was his protégé) at sea; therefore he was sent to the West Indies to take Hispaniola. Not having been able to succeed in that enterprise, which was, one may say, the only thing Cromwell had to give up trying to do, he turned to Jamaica with better success in order not to return without having done anything. He was at all the battles fought against the Dutch in Cromwell's time, in the

---

[69] Sir Edward Spragge (d. 1673).
[70] Sir John Kempthorne (1620–1679).
[71] Sir Thomas Allin (1612–1685).
[72] Sir John Harman (d. 1673).
[73] This Sir William Penn (1621–1670) was not the Quaker who founded Pennsylvania, but his father. There are many references to him in Pepys' *Diary*.

post of Vice-Admiral. Now he has been knighted for services rendered to the King in his restoration as well as in these latest battles; and today he is the favourite protégé of the Duke, who, if he ever goes to sea, will take him with him as Vice-Admiral. These appointments vary according to circumstances and the pleasure of the King, that is to say the officers in them.

Sir George Ayscue,[74] of noble family, has always followed the fortunes of Sandwich. He was with him at Teneriffe and in the Sound, and consequently he also contributed to the return of the king, being at that time Vice-Admiral of the fleet under Sandwich as Admiral. In Cromwell's time he was in supreme command of a squadron of ships sent to help the Swedes, for which he was generously rewarded by that king. In the second battle he was made Admiral of the white and commanded the *Royal Prince,* which in the midst of the battle went on a shoal, and was at once attacked by Dutch fireships, so that the vessel was set on fire and he was taken prisoner. According to the naval rules observed in the kingdom, he should have set his ship on fire although it was aground, and because he did not do so, he was so much in disgrace with the King that he let him remain a prisoner in Holland for eighteen months,[75] although he could have freed him in a fortnight with one word. He would still be there but for the conclusion of peace. The laws of the sea in England oblige the captain of a ship to fight against three inferior vessels or two similar ones; from a greater number they are allowed to sail away. The penalty exacted for not observing these laws is to have his sword broken on his head by a great blow in public on a platform.

Sir Frescheville Holles,[76] a blood relation of Lord Holles, commands the fireships in time of war. This appointment is conferred on a person of great experience and courage, and the commander always goes on the largest fireship. This gentleman lost an arm in the second battle, so that as a recompense he was knighted and got a company in Monk's regiment. He is a young man of thirty, did not serve Cromwell, and is a protégé of the General, who himself is a naval officer with flag rank, and also raises his flag on a fireship.

---

[74] Sir George Ayscue (fl. 1646–1671). Pepys (Tanner, *Descriptive Catalogue,* 1, 313) would have him Vice-Admiral of the blue at that time.

[75] Really about sixteen months.

[76] Sir Frescheville Holles (1641–1672). He was related to John Holles. Earl of Clare. Pepys had a poor opinion of him.

Sir John Jennings,[77] who commanded the fireships when the Dutch came to Chatham, is a soldier of good reputation and a protégé of the Duke.

Among ship captains the following are in high esteem: Sir Francis Digby,[78] second son of the Earl of Bristol, twenty-five years old. Captain Utber;[79] at the beginning of the late war he was a flag officer, but then renounced his commission because of advanced age. He is of good family and a high reputation in the navy. Captain O'Brien, son of the Earl of Inchiquin,[80] an Irishman and a Catholic; in all the battles of the recent war he showed great courage and good conduct. The King is very fond of him and regards him as a man to make a great soldier of. This year he is to be with the fleet. Sidney[81] is a young man of twenty-three, rich and noble; even though he is the eldest son of his house, he went to sea to get reputation and esteem, and succeeded so well that he was later made a captain and knighted. Lord Bellamont, First Lieutenant of the *Sovereign,* is a young man of twenty-two who is trying to make his fortune in the military, and has now gone to the West Indies with a regiment of infantry. Almost all the other captains are soldiers of fortune.

Pay of the Officers and Soldiers of the Fleet[82]

Admirals, two pounds sterling a day, and when they are at sea they are provided by the King with subsistence for all the volunteers and officers. Vice-Admirals, a pound and a half, with subsistence. Rear-Admirals, one pound, with subsistence. Captains of

---

[77] It is possible that there is a confusion with Sir William Jennens, promoted to captain of the *Ruby* in 1664 and later commissioned to other ships.

[78] Francis Digby had various commissions as captain. W. A. Shaw, *The Knights of England* (London, 1906) makes no reference to a knighthood.

[79] Richard Utber (Crinò). I have been able to find no information about him.

[80] Murrough O'Brien, sixth Baron Inchiquin and first Earl (1614–1674). The Captain was Charles O'Brien, promoted in 1665 (Tanner, *Descriptive Catalogue,* 1, 388).

[81] Sidney: Pepys does not list him (Tanner, *Descriptive Catalogue*).

[82] Tanner (*Descriptive Catalogue,* 1, 140) gives the following list for flag officers:

vice-admiral of the fleet, 50 shillings a day
rear-admiral of the fleet, 40 shillings a day
vice-admiral of a squadron, 30 shillings a day
rear-admiral of a squadron, 20 shillings a day.

second-rates, fifteen shillings a day.Captains of third-rates, twelve shillings. Captains of fourth-rates, ten shillings. Captains of fifth-rates (the last), eight shillings, like captains of infantry on land.

As soon as they are afloat by the King's command all the captains of the fleet have subsistence, not in money but in provisions furnished by the King's victuallers. Their other gifts from the King are when ships are captured: all the equipment of the enemy and everything below decks except guns and cordage.

Lieutenants of large vessels, six shillings a day; of medium ships, four; of the lesser ships, two. Mariners, ten pence a day. Soldiers, eight.

The King furnishes the entire fleet with provisions, so that they all have subsistence. The officers, both great and small, are on half-pay when they are not actually in the royal service, either in peace or in war. The soldiers and sailors get nothing. However, these are not distressed by peace, because they earn much more in traffic with the Indies and in the pay they get from the merchants in whose service they make voyages.

List of Vessels that the English Admit Losing in the Recent War

The *Charity*, sunk in the first battle; and they say that it was the only one lost there. It carried 40 guns. The *Hector*, said to have been lost in a storm when Sandwich took the Dutch vessels of the Indies fleet. They say it was very old; 46 guns. The *Essex*, a very fine vessel; 60 guns. The *Swiftsure*, commanded by Barclay; 60 guns. They assert that these last two were the only ones lost in the second battle at the hands of the enemy. The *Royal Prince*, commanded by Sir George Ayscue, went aground during the battle and was set on fire by fireships; 80 guns. Besides these three last vessels lost, there were seven or eight burned and sent to the bottom, but all these had been taken from the Dutch on other occasions, and came to grief by being exposed to greater risks as being of lesser account.

When the English are asked what happened in the second battle, in which each side believed itself victorious, they answer that the reciprocal mistake arose because besides the above-mentioned ten of their vessels that were lost, all the rest of the fleet was in great disorder and many vessels left and retired towards the coast of England for repairs. From this disorder and absence the Dutch argue the defeat of the fleet to have been much greater than it was. On the other hand, the Dutch entered the battle with 100 sail and came out of it after four days of conflict with forty, because many were scattered over the sea, and this enabled the English to think that the others were all lost; and so, from this mutual mistake is said to have been derived the vain belief of each side that it had entirely defeated the enemy.

In the third and last battle they swear that the *Old Resolution* was the only vessel burned and lost. In the Chatham affair, according to the English, only the *Royal Charles,* captured and taken away. As to this vessel, it is said to have been agreed secretly, or rather all English sailors have sworn, that they will try to recapture it wherever they find it outside of Dutch ports, with no regard to the peace. The *Royal James,* the *Loyal London,* and the *Royal Oak* were burned and the rebuilding of all of them has now been begun. It seems to me that "oak" is the name of a kind of tree and that the vessel is so called from the tree in which the present King hid after the defeat of his people in Scotland, but I am not sure that I am not mistaken. These were burned while trying to defend the chain that guarded the port and all three had been taken from the Dutch on other occasions.

This is how many they admit were lost on that occasion, and they are angry with anyone who says there were more. Another English vessel called the *St. Patrick,* of fifty guns, they confess to having lost in the following way: they say that during the winter it met with two Dutch vessels and fought with them. The captain, the lieutenant, and sixty soldiers were killed, and the remainder surrendered instead of setting the ship on fire.

List of Warships Taken from the Dutch in the Recent War

One, before the first battle, taken like the *St. Patrick*; the son of Evertsen[83] was aboard her. Twelve taken in the Duke of York's battle, and seven sent to the bottom. Eight by Sandwich in the north. Thirteen in the second battle, but all sent to the bottom and none captured. Two in the third and last battle, both large and well armed: one from the Admiral of Holland, Evertsen, who died aboard, and the other from Vice-Admiral Bauchaert, who was saved. The English captured them, but found them so badly damaged that they were obliged to sink them. Four warships burned among those many merchantmen at Vlie.

---

[83] Cornelis Evertsen (1610–1666) (Crinò).

List of Warships Taken from the French

The *Ruby*, 60 guns; the *Victoire*, 30 guns. The English vessels, then, now in the hands of the Dutch are four: the *Royal Charles*, the *Essex*, the *Swiftsure*, and the *St. Patrick*. The law about setting ships on fire rather than surrendering them is the reason that they have so few, and these few surrendered after the deaths of their captains, except the *Royal Charles* which (according to them) they tried three times to set on fire, but there was not enough powder to blow her up.

English warships burned and sunk 14
English warships, captured 4
Total losses 18
French warships captured 2
Total losses 2

List of the English Fleet, According to the Description Issued at the End of March, 1668[84]

First-rates	Men	Guns
Royal Sovereign	900	104
Royal Charles	900	106
Royal Prince	900	110
Royal James	600	90

Second-rates		
Royal Catherine	500	80
Old James	500	82
Loyal London	500	80
Royal Oak	520	80
Victory	450	80
Triumph	430	74
St. George	400	70
Unicorn	450	76
Cambridge	400	70
St. Andrew	360	66
Rainbow	350	60

---

[84] I have checked this list against the one compiled by R. C. Anderson, *Lists of Men-of-war, 1650–1700. Part I: English Ships, 1649–1702*, 2nd ed. (Society for Nautical Research, Occasional Publications, no. 5) (London, 1966). I was able to verify all the first-, second-, and third-rates, most of the fourth- and fifth-rates. From the remarks in this reference I should judge that Magalotti had a list dating from 1666 or early in 1667.

	Men	Guns
Vanguard	330	60
Henry	300	60
Happy Return	300	60
Ruby (French)	300	60

Third-rates

Monmouth	350	60
Revenge	300	58
Coventry	320	64
Henrietta	300	60
Defiance	320	68
Monk	280	56
Fairfax	300	64
Slothany	280	60
Mary	300	64
Anne	280	60
Rupert	320	66
Plymouth	280	58
York	280	58
Helverston (Dutch)	300	60
Dreadnought	300	60
Gloucester	280	60
Warspite	350	66
Golden Phoenix	280	60
House of Sweden (Dutch)	280	60
Resolution (burned)	300	64
Lion	300	60
Montagu	300	60

Fourth-rates

Princess	250	54
Ruby	200	50
Catherine	200	48
Crown	220	48
Providence	200	48
Convention	230	52
Matthias (Dutch)	220	54
Jersey	180	46
Marmaduke	160	44
Westfriesland (Dutch)	180	50
Diamond	180	48

	Men	Guns
Jonathan (Dutch)	160	46
Gelderland (Dutch)	180	48
Breda (Dutch)	180	48
Zeeland (Dutch)	160	46
Expedition	150	42
Baltimore	150	50
Security	150	44
Dover	170	50
Falcon	150	46
Greenwich	150	46
Leopard	250	56
Centurion	180	50
Faithful Subject	150	48
Mary Rose	180	52
Black Eagle (Dutch)	180	48
Hampshire	160	42
Faithful George	160	42
St. Mary (Dutch)	180	50
St. Paul (Dutch)	160	42
Seven Chains (Dutch)	190	52
Friendship (Dutch)	150	48
Warning	180	48
Yarmouth	200	48
Unity (Dutch)	150	42
Good Fortune	180	48
Society (Dutch)	150	40
Soranero (Dutch)	150	40
Welcome	150	40
Constant Warwick	150	40
Elizabeth	170	44
Sapphire	150	48
Newcastle	200	52
Reserve	180	50
Antelope	180	48
Assistance (Dutch)	150	40
Portland	200	50
Portsmouth	180	48
Bristol	170	46
Dragon	156	40
Kent	180	48
Guinea	150	40

Fifth-rates	Guns
Fortune	38
Sweepstakes	36
Providence	38
Sorlinges	36
Richmond	30
Nightingale	32
Dartmouth	30
Oxford	28
Pearl	28
Paul	30
Paradox	20
Drake	20
Fox	16
Guernsey	28
Great Don	36
Mermaid	30
Milford	30
Hunter	30
Guardland	28
Little Victory	24
Success	32
Orange	26
Martino	14
Pembroke	32
Colchester	28
Speedwell	28
Norwich	28
Little Mary	14
Eagle	32

These fifth-rates are not counted among the ships of the fleet, for they are not warships of the King but of private men, such as corsairs or merchants, and serve only on the more important occasions, as happened in this latest war with Holland. Besides these there are the capers and the fireships. The capers are small vessels of four to ten guns that in time of war go in the fleet and take orders from the admiral without any dependence on the King. There are moreover various small warships that have gone to the Indies to convoy merchant ships, of which one cannot precisely find out the number. In times of need the larger vessels of the Indies trade arm themselves for war and carry as many as forty or fifty guns. New ships are always being built to maintain the number, more than ever now, in proportion to the losses, which have been greater.

In peacetime the King always maintains a small squadron of warships called the Guard of St. George's channel or the English channel, for the security of the strait. He does this at his own expense, having a special allowance for it. When the King needs to build more ships or arm a larger fleet than usual, he asks Parliament for additional money.

The commissions of the officers of the fleet are not attached to particular people, but are at the disposal of the King, so that those who will go out this year are not exactly the same men who had commands in the recent war and who are described in this report.

Status of the English Court

The Court of the King

Charles II the king.

Grand Constable. This office was formerly permanent, but now is not conferred except for a limited time, and that very short. One of the reasons for this is the excessive authority that it retains by reason of its first establishment, by which it has rights over the entire realm, so that in a certain way it puts the royal dignity itself in the shade. Nowadays it seems that the reason for conferring it comes uniquely either from the needs of the judicature of the Peers and Barons of the Realm, or from solemn functions such as the coronation of kings and queens, marriages and other public solemnities. During the period of his office the Grand Constable carries in hand a white staff about the height of a man, with which he supports himself while walking.

High Admiral, James, Duke of York, the King's only brother.

The Archbishop of Canterbury, Primate of England.

The Lord Chancellor was formerly Edward Hyde, Earl of Clarendon. This office has the use of the great seal and general supervision over all civil and criminal justice.

Lord High Treasurer. This office is vacant because of the death of Lord Southampton, and is at present conducted by four[85] men appointed by the King, of whom mention was made elsewhere. But it should be known that the general treasury furnishes all the other treasuries of the King, all the royal income that flows into it being registered in the master account books, kept with the greatest punctuality and exactness by the Lord High Treasurer's clerks, who are subject to the most rigorous audit of their accounts. He pays the militia and every other household expense, the officers of the King and of the crown, except those who are paid by other treasurers subordinate to him. These are the Privy Purse, the one called that of the Household, the Treasury of

---

[85] There were in fact five. See p. 52 above.

the navy, and the Wardrobe. The first pays everything that is ordered to be paid by way of pensions, offices, extra payments, and other special headings; and it usually has so much a month from the great treasury. The second pays all those officers who depend on the high steward, who corresponds to the *maiordomo maggiore* of the Italian courts. The third pays everything necessary for the armament of the fleet. The last is entirely for the use of the King for his pleasures. To these is added in time of war the Treasury of Prizes, which receives the King's orders for the employment of the funds received from the sale of those prizes. In addition there are the separate paymasters of the guards, both horse and foot, each of which has its own separate treasurer.

Keeper of the Seals, Lord Bridgeman.[86] This is a kind of office under the Chancellor. Keeper of the Private Seal, Lord Robartes.

Grand Marshal. This office is hereditary in the family of the Dukes of Norfolk, but now it is vacant because this branch is Catholic, so that they cannot take the oath recognizing the King as head of the church, independent of the Pope. The Grand Marshal has jurisdiction over all the nobility, deciding all cases concerning matters of honour and chivalry, whether they are disputes about precedence, or a criminal charge, or inquiries, or a duel. But it is an honorary office with no emoluments.

Lord Chamberlain, the Earl of Lindsey,[87] in whose family this office is hereditary. This one is also merely one of show and is not visible except on occasions of public and extraordinary solemnity. He carries a white staff.

General George Monk, Duke of Albermarle, Master of the Horse.

The above-mentioned Chamberlain of the King, Edward Montagu, Earl of Manchester, corresponds to the *maestro di camera*. He carries a white staff and a gold key at his side, attached to a dark blue ribbon.

Under-chamberlain, Sir George Cartaret, an office dependent on the Chamberlain.

Lord Steward of the Household James Butler, Duke of Ormonde. He carries a white staff.

---

[86] This was Sir Orlando Bridgeman (ca. 1606–1674), the Lord Keeper. He was given the great seal on Clarendon's dismissal but not the office of Chancellor.

[87] Robert Bertie, Earl of Lindsey (ca. 1630–1701).

Comptroller of the Household, Viscount Fitzharding, of the Berkeley family. He carries a white staff.

Under-Comptroller, Sir Thomas Clifford. He carries a white staff.

First Gentleman of the Bedchamber, the Earl of Bath, of the Grenville family. He carries a golden key.

Gentlemen of the Bedchamber: these are usually the foremost of the realm.

First Secretary of State, Lord Arlington.

Secretary of State, Sir William Morice.

Chancellor of the Treasury, Lord Ashley; he is under the Lord High Treasurer and is his principal assistant.

Treasurer of the Navy, the Earl of Anglesey. He administers all the money for arming and maintaining the fleet.

Secretary of the Navy, Mr. Wrenn[88]; he is under the Lord High Admiral.

Captain of the Pensioners' Guard, Lord Belasyse.

Captain of the Yeomen of the Guard, Lord Grandison.

The Queen's Court

Catherine, Princess of Portugal, Queen of England.

Grand Almoner, Lord Philip Howard, brother of the Duke of Norfolk.

Chamberlain: the office is suspended. Lord Cornbury,[89] eldest son of the above-mentioned chancellor, had it. It is thought that the Earl of Sunderland, of the Sidney[90] family, might get it. He is a Gentleman of the King's Bedchamber. This office carries with it the golden key.

Groom of the Bedchamber, Killigrew.[91] He carries the golden key.

Master of the Horse, Montagu.[92]

Secretary, Sir Richard Bellings.[93]

---

[88] Matthew Wrenn (1629–1672); not to be confused with the great architect.

[89] Henry Hyde (1638–1709), Viscount Cornbury, later second Earl of Clarendon.

[90] Robert Spencer (1641–1702), third Earl of Sunderland. He was not, of course, of the Sidney family.

[91] Thomas Killigrew (1613–1683), a dramatist and courtier who in 1663 built a playhouse in Drury Lane. At the time of Magalotti's visit he was the official court jester (Pepys' *Diary*, February 13, 1667/8).

[92] Ralph Montagu, Duke of Montagu (ca. 1638–1709).

[93] Sir Richard Bellings, son of the Irish historian Richard Bellings.

First Lady-in-Waiting, the Countess of Suffolk. She carries a golden key.

Under her are the ladies-in-waiting, who are the chief ladies of the realm and all married, after whom come the maids-of-honour, who have to be girls; these have quarters in Whitehall.

Court of the Queen Mother

Grand Almoner, Lord Montagu,[94] brother of the Earl of Manchester. The latter is a Presbyterian, the former a Catholic.

Chamberlain, Henry Jermyn, Earl of St. Albans.

Master of the Horse, Lord Arundell,[95] which is a family name, not a title, as in the Howard family.

Secretary, Sir John Winter.

First Lady-in-Waiting, the Dowager Duchess of Richmond, remarried to a young man of the Howard family. She is the sister of the Duke of Buckingham and aunt of the present Duke of Richmond.

Court of the Duke of York

First gentleman of the Bedchamber, the Marquis of Blanquefort,[96] a Frenchman of the Duras family, nephew of Marshall Turenne and also Keeper of the Duke's Privy Purse.

Master of the Horse, Henry Jermyn, nephew and heir of the Earl of St. Albans.

---

[94] Walter Montagu (ca. 1603–1677), Abbot of St. Martin's, near Pontoise. He was not a lord.

[95] Henry Arundell (ca. 1606–1694), third Baron Arundell of Wardour.

[96] See note 19, p. 79.

On the Nobility of England in General

There are three classes into which the different sorts of people in England are divided, the patricians, the knightly order, and the common people, called in English *Noblemen, gentry, yeomen*.

Patricians and noblemen are all those who are barons, under which title pass indiscriminately the dukes, the marquesses, the earls and the viscounts. Between these the pre-eminence of the title makes no difference except in the order of precedence, while otherwise being a baron is alone what gives them a place in Parliament and gives them all the other privileges of peers of the realm, the chief of which is that they cannot be judged in criminal cases except by their own body. In such a case the King names a constable and deputizes as many barons as he pleases, and the impartiality of none of these can be suspected, even if he should be a principal enemy of the accused. The latter sits at the Bar with his legal advisers on one side, and the witnesses for the prosecution on the other. There are also some of the legal profession called *siure*, [1] who interpret the laws when this is needed, and after the interpretation the sentence is pronounced, after which the constable breaks the white staff that he holds in his hand, and this means that his authority and his office have expired.

On the particular forms of this judicature I refer to Camden, [2] to Smith, [3] and to others who have written *ex professo* about English matters and about the customs of the kingdom.

The title of marquis, earl, or baron does not of itself include being a peer, and in fact there are many who have titles and are not peers. He only is a peer who is declared to be so by the King. This means that outside of Parliament a duke, although he may not be a peer, precedes an earl who is one; but in Parliament not only does

---

[1] This is probably an attempt at writing the word "jury". Magalotti seems confused about the procedure; the lords can of course avail themselves of the opinion of eminent legal talent.

[2] William Camden (1551–1623), author of *Britannia* (London, 1586).

[3] Sir Thomas Smith (1513–1577) wrote *De republica Anglorum* (London, 1583).

he not precede him, but as mentioned, he has not even a place there.[4] All the eldest sons of peers enter Parliament to become skilled in knowledge of the laws and the affairs of the kingdom, but have neither deliberative nor consultative power.

The eldest sons of dukes are all earls; the others, that is the second and younger sons, are, with a certain impartiality, called *lord* as long as they live, but if they marry they do not pass the title to their children. The same applies to the children of marquesses, but the eldest sons of earls are called viscounts and the younger ones *esquire*. Finally the eldest sons of viscounts and of barons are all *esquires*; the children of dukes, as earls, do not take relative precedence in the same order as their fathers, that is to say according to the creation of the dukedoms, but according to that of the earldoms of which they bear the titles. Finally they have to be peers in order to vote and are seated according to the inequality of title, and among equals according to the creation of that title. It is also to be noted that all the children of noblemen, the eldest-born as well as the younger, are comprised in the class of *noblemen,* and for that reason precede all those classed as *gentry,* or knightly men, as one might say.

The knightly order includes all those who by royal privilege or by custom compose this class, which is divided into baronets, Knights of the Bath, Knights of the Garter, golden knights, squires, and gentlemen.[5] The Knights of the Bath are created only at the King's coronation and at the proclamation of the Prince of Wales and are for the most part sons of the nobility; they sit according to the order of birth without any regard to the precedence of the knightly class, of which their order of chivalry is made up. Their firstborn are *squires,* and have the same rules of precedence as their fathers. The women in the same way. The other children are all gentlemen, and have the same precedence as the eldest sons.

The *yeomen* are all the common people, rich and poor.[6]

The daughters of dukes, marquesses, earls, and barons are called *Lady* and have precedence in the same order as their fathers, whence all the women in England have the precedence of their

---

[4] Magalotti has not understood the system.

[5] The last two classes are not knights. "Golden knights" (*cavalieri aurati*) seems to be a translation of *equites aurati*, i.e. knights.

[6] This is Magalotti's most conspicuous error. It was well that no English yeoman had the opportunity of reading this.

younger brothers, as there is not primogeniture among them. The others are all *Mistress,* which [in Italian] is simply *signora*. All the ladies are generally called *Madam*, especially when they are beautiful, but strictly this form of address should go only to queens and princesses of the blood, and in this connection it should be observed that in England, only those who are children and grandchildren of kings are called princes and princesses of the blood. Up to this rank they precede all the other people of title either ecclesiastical or temporal, but from there on they are considered only according to the quality of their titles. Thus the grandsons of the Duke of York will sit in Parliament below the sons of the living Duke of Norfolk.

The King is addressed only as *Sire*.

Dukes and archbishops are given the title of *Grace,* when speaking of them in the third person, or *Most Honourable,* but this second one is not too much in use. Some people, for a whim or out of self-interest or in flattery, also give this title to marquesses.

In writing to earls down to barons it is usual to call them *Right Honourable,* that is to say justly[7] honourable. To those Councillors of State that are neither dukes, nor marquesses, nor earls, nor barons, to secretaries of state, baronets and other knights one writes *Honourable,* and if speaking in the third person, *Your Honour,* and to barons, viscounts, and earls, *Your Lordship*.

Ecclesiastical titles are of three kinds. To deans, canons, priests, ministers, and doctors, *Reverend Father*; to bishops *Right Reverend Father*; to archbishops *Most Reverend Father*. To the last I have already said that in the third person you say *Your Grace*.

The title of princes of the blood is *Illustrious,* or *Most Illustrious,* which is also given to the king with the other titles *Sovereign* and *Most Gracious*. The title for writing to the King is *To the King's Most Excellent Majesty,* or *Most Serene* in exchange for *Most Excellent,* which is equivalent to *serenissima*. I think that the English nation is the only one that gives its king the title of "Excellency."

I said at the beginning of these memoirs that in respect to his subjects the King of England is simply the source of grace and honour and in fact all the nobility are so called because of his indulgence and privilege. About the first rank, which includes the barons and peers of the realm, and the second, which comprises the baronets and knights, there is no doubt. The third, to which

---

[7] Miss Crinò correctly informs her readers that it means "very honourable."

belong the squires and all those who call themselves gentlemen, is also of the same nature as the other two. It is quite true that use and custom give them those names even without the express and particular declaration of the King. It results from this, that the merit of noble blood alone is not held in any esteem unless a title or post that is worthy of respect gives it a new lustre, and thus the younger sons and the sons of younger sons of the first families of the kingdom serve as slaves to their eldest brothers and of those of the descendents of the head of their families. The most necessitous make no difficulty about actually serving as secretaries, house-stewards, tutors of boys, and even valets. Simple private knights will even put their sons to serve masters of the lowest trades such as tailors, shoemakers, innkeepers, and in every other business of a similar kind. Thus we see young men of the noblest blood mixing with the lowest classes without being distinguished by their clothes or anything else. From this results the confusion of the great houses, since because the prerogative of titles prevails over nobility of blood, it becomes difficult to retrace the real aristocracy and to be able to discern it among the splendour of dignities and offices.

I shall go on to record some of the principal families, nevertheless making it clear that I am observing no other order than the one in which they come to mind.

The first of all the realm are, beyond any contradiction, Howard and Savile. The former, besides its ancient nobility, is to the highest degree remarkable for the number of titles that it has above any other family, since besides those of Duke of Norfolk, Earl of Arundel and Baron Maltravers, who were the first duke, earl, and baron of the kingdom,[8] it counts at least seven other earldoms in seven other branches.

The main branch is that of the Dukes of Norfolk and the Earls of Arundel, united in the person of the present Duke,[9] who for many years has lived, mad, at Padua. He is a Catholic. The income is at present enjoyed by the second son, who now only lives as a simple knight, but as a knight whom nothing but the existence of a madman keeps from showing himself as the second personage of the kingdom after the King. He has two sons, the older sixteen,

---

[8] One Ralph was created Earl of Norfolk by William the Conqueror. He died ca. 1069. The dukedom dates from 1397, but entered the Howard family by marriage in 1483.

[9] Thomas Howard (1627–1677). His brother was Henry Howard (1628–1684), sixth Duke of Norfolk after 1677. (CP)

the younger thirteen years old, both very handsome. The father thinks that at some time he will divide between them the titles united in their uncle, duke and earl, his income of 26,000 pounds sterling being quite sufficient to make two houses great.

These two boys have been at school in Paris for several years under the direction of a wise and virtuous Catholic gentleman called Sir Samuel Tuke,[10] who has just retired from their service. The father is disposed to send them to Christ's College at Oxford for two years and then take them with him to Italy.

He is a widower, but lives with a very beautiful woman,[11] with whom he fell in love many years ago, the first time he saw her. Others had already possessed her, and especially the Duke of Buckingham. However he at once had him sent on his way. As his love increased, the brothers suspected that his excessive passion would drive him to marry her, and begged the King to caution him seriously. The King did this, and they say that he threatened to take his revenues and have them administered by a custodian of his brother. To escape from the toils of love he made a journey to Constantinople at the moment when Count Leslie[12] went there as ambassador for the emperor, but he kept the fire burning by way of a continual exchange of letters. Scarcely had he returned when he brought her back to England from a convent in Flanders where he had left her. At present he keeps her in London, sleeps there regularly three times a week and has had a son by her.[13] Since she has been in his hands she has lived very prudently. Indeed he does not forget to keep her very well watched. However, he is thinking of bringing her to the vicinity of his country house, building her a villa on the Thames that he can go to through his garden. The brother,[14] who is the Grand Almoner of the Queen, a man of exemplariness worthy of an ecclesiastic, torments him without cease, but he defends himself with great self-possession.

The other family, Savile, which claims to be a branch of the Savelli of Rome, is of great antiquity and riches. It is divided into two main branches: the first that of the Earls of Sussex, and the other that of the Viscounts of Halifax, with a very large number of knights and gentlemen.

---

[10] Sir Samuel Tuke (d. 1674) was also a playwright.

[11] Jane Bickerton, whose father Robert was gentleman of the wine cellar to the King. Henry Howard eventually married her, but not until 1678 (*CP*).

[12] Walter Leslie (1606–1667). He had a German title.

[13] He finally had four sons and three daughters by her.

[14] Philip Thomas Howard (1629–1694) known as Cardinal of Norfolk.

The Duke of Somerset is of the Seymour family, a very old one. It seems to me that it obtained the title from Henry VIII after he had married one of its women.[15]

The Duke of Buckingham, of the Villiers family, got the title in the person of his father,[16] with those of Marquess, Earl, and Baron by the favour of King James, by whom he was tenderly loved in the finest flower of his youth. He also obtained the title of Earl of Anglesey for a brother, who had no descendants.[17] Now that house has an annual income of more than 20,000 pounds.

The Duke of Richmond: his family became English about sixty years ago; a few years before that time they were called the Dukes of Lennox, a Scottish title. It comes from a Seigneur d'Aubigny of a family that lived for many generations in France, and had had its origin in the Scottish family Stuart and came to be the closest relation (although still very remote) that King James had. For that reason he recalled the seigneur from France and gave him an English dukedom and made a great man of him, as his relation.[18] The present Duke, a very young man, has the titles of Admiral and Lord Chamberlain of Scotland, and is a Knight of the Garter and a Gentleman of the Bedchamber to the king. His wealth, however, is not in proportion to his condition or his offices, for it was dissipated by the wars and by the ostentatious prodigality of his uncle, part of whose estate he inherited. He is the son of a younger brother, the elder having died without having had an heir by his wife, the sister of the present Duke of Buckingham.

I have already spoken of the family of the Duke of Albemarle when speaking of that Duke himself. I will now add that in the short time that has elapsed since the restoration of the King he is reckoned to have got an income of 20,000 pounds a year. Shortly before I arrived in England he had bought a broad estate with a very beautiful country house from the Duke of Buckingham, yielding an income of more than 4,000 pounds a year.

---

[15] Jane Seymour (ca. 1509–1537), third Queen of Henry VIII. Her brother, Edward, was later created Duke of Somerset.

[16] George Villiers (1592–1628), favourite of James I, who made him the first Duke of Buckingham.

[17] Christopher Villiers (*ca.* 1593–1630) had a son, Charles, who became the second Earl of Anglesey, and whose stepdaughter was Barbara, Countess of Castlemaine.

[18] Ludovick Stuart (1574–1624), second Duke of Lennox, made Duke of Richmond in 1623 by James I.

I have also discussed the Dukes of Ormonde and Monmouth elsewhere, so that I pass on to the Duke of Newcastle[19] and say that he is the head of the cadet branch of the Cavendish family, which is said to be very ancient. The head of the family is the Earl of Devonshire, Viscount and Baron Cavendish,[20] a man who begins to be old, but a very fine and cordial gentleman. He and his cousin, the Duke of Newcastle, are considered to be among the oldest lords in England and between them are calculated to have an income of over 50,000 pounds a year.

The Earl of Devonshire has two children, the older of whom is the most dissolute man in London and gets on badly with his father. He has a daughter of the Duke of Ormonde for a wife, and she is very beautiful. The younger is a boy of twelve or thirteen. The Countess of Devonshire,[21] the Earl's mother, is still living in a magnificent house in the style of something more than a great princess. She is over eighty-six and is of a stature that would be formidable in a man, let alone a woman. She has gentlemen for servants, and sets a sumptuous table every day. Her house is always full of visitors. Her apartment is full of precious articles of furniture and silver. She lies upon a bed placed on an island after the French manner, under a sort of canopy, from the frame of which hangings go down to the floor, which would close like bed-curtains if it were not that being open and drawn aside here and there they form the canopy of a tabernacle rather than that of a bed. The Countess does not move nor get up unless she is supported on the arms of two very lovely damsels. Her eighty-seven years and the paralysis that she has in her neck, so that her head always turns round like the balance wheel of a watch, do not stop her wearing under-petticoats of materials adorned with flower patterns in bright colours and large amounts of silver lace.

[They tell me that the Earl's wife amuses herself merrily.] What [the Earl's wife][22] may do I do not know, but I hear that her four sisters all amuse themselves gallantly. I will recount a ridicul-

---

[19] William Cavendish (1592–1676).
[20] William Cavendish (1617–1684).
[21] Christiana, Countess of Devonshire (1595–1675). She was really only about seventy-three when Magalotti was in England. She was in the habit of entertaining the "wits and men of letters," and seems to have been very greatly respected. The "magnificent house" was at Roehampton.
[22] The passages in brackets were decoded by Miss Crinò from Magalotti's cipher.

ous incident about one of them, who is married to[23] . . . One day she was in the new Exchange with a knight, one of her friends, to provide herself with knick-knacks. They began to talk about hopping on one foot, and she said she would dare to hop along the whole central corridor of the Exchange from one end to the other. The knight said she would not; she said she would; finally they made a large bet. The lady, raising her skirts a little (the Exchange was full as it always is) did as she had said she would. Angry at losing, the knight ran after her, took her in his arms and, laying her on a table in one of the shops, face downwards, lifted up her skirts and gave her half a dozen spanks without any consequences for himself other than paying his bet.

I was forgetting that the Duke of Newcastle is called both Marquess and Duke at the same time and possesses by inheritance the earldom of Ogle and the viscounty of Mansfield, but without having a single foot of land in either place.

The Marquess of Winchester is of the Paulet family; the Marquess of Worcester is a Herbert; the Marquess of Dorchester is of the Pierreponts; all three very good families.

Among the earls, after the Earl of Arundel, who as I said above is of the Howard family, comes the Earl of Oxford of the de Veres, a very ancient family.

The Earl of Shrewsbury is of the house of Talbot, a family also as old as any other in England.

The Earl of Northumberland is of the house of Percy, a rich, great, and ancient family that because it claims descent from the house of Lorraine boasts of imaginary rights to the crown of France on account of the usurpation of Hugh Capet. With these visions is always associated the name Algernon, which was that of the Duke of Lorraine of their branch, who at that time should have succeeded to the throne.

The Earl of Kent is of the house of Grey, ancient but not very wealthy.

The Earl of Bedford is of the Russell family, who claim to have come from Italy, from some place or other in Lombardy. Some people say yes, some say no. This happens with the greater part of the families of England, about the antiquity of which there are the most various opinions. Whatever may be the nobility of this house, nobody disagrees that it is very rich, even in fact one of the richest in the kingdom. The income from the houses that the

---

[23] A lacuna in the manuscript.

Earl has in London, all together in the district called Covent Garden, almost all of which is his property, is alone valued at about 10,000 pounds a year.

The Earls of Manchester and of Sandwich, both very rich, are of the Montagu family, which is certainly among the most noble. They claim to be the same as the Montauti of Tuscany. The principal branch has the title of Baron. The Earl of Manchester is also Earl of Mandeville.

The Earl of Warwick is of the house of Rich, an old family that has had the title for a very long time.

The Earl of Suffolk is of a branch of the Howard family, and not very wealthy. The Earl of Carlisle is from another branch of the same house; this man too was only of slight wealth, but it seems to me that I have heard that since his return from his embassy in Denmark he has saved much ready money.

The Earl of Berkshire is from another branch of the same family, less rich than the two preceding, and gravely harmed by the recent wars.

The Earl of Salisbury is from the house of Cecil, a family that came up in the time of Queen Elizabeth with the great riches accumulated by his grandfather and his grandfather's brother, the former, High Treasurer, the latter, Prime Minister.[24] The Earl of Exeter, of the above family, is descended from the Prime Minister.

The Earl of Strafford of the old and very rich family of Wentworth. It is well known how the father of this Earl was decapitated in the time of the late King, who for his own security was obliged to sacrifice him to the hate of Parliament, marking his sentence of death with the most unrestrained tears, as for one whom he knew for his best friend, innocent of all the crimes imputed to him.

The Earl of Newport [is] of the house of Mountjoy, an old and rich family. These are also among those who claim to have come from France with William the Conqueror. I have never found any sensible people who allow either to them or to others the proofs of this conjectured truth.

The Earl of Pembroke and Montgomery, of the Herbert family, [is] very well-off. The Earl of Sunderland of the house of

---

[24] Magalotti is referring to William Cecil, Lord Burghley (1520–1598) and his son (*not* his brother), Robert Cecil, first Earl of Salisbury (*ca.* 1563–1613). Lord Burghley did not, in fact, leave a great fortune, as he had lived in a princely fashion, but he passed considerable property on to his son Thomas, Earl of Exeter, who, however, "died owing nearly £38,000" (*DNB*).

Sidney, a family of very good repute. The Earl of Westmorland of the house of Fane has a new title, but the family is supposed to be ancient. The Earl of Bristol [is] of the house of Digby, also a new title, but not a new family. Viscount Paget, a very good house.

The house of Berkeley is also very old. It has two barons and a viscount. The first of the barons and the viscount are called Baron and Viscount of Berkeley, the second Baron Fitzharding, father of the Earl of Falmouth who died in the first battle when his vessel was taken by the Dutch.

The two families of Huntington and Derby slipped my mind. Both have the titles of Earl. The second has also the title of King of the Isle of Man. These families are important because of marriages with royalty or for their rivalry with the realm in the time of King James.

There would be things to say about many others, and perhaps I have neglected some of the most illustrious in favour of some less considerable. Now, in fact, I remember the Spencer family, perhaps as noble as any other that I have named, but this may be condoned as the ignorance of a foreigner who remained for the space of only two months in such a great court, at which he had arrived entirely unprovided with information or friends.

The Lower House, or House of Commons

The first parliamentarians of the lower house, called knights of the shire, are elected as follows. In the thirty-two counties into which England is divided, all those who have a certain specified wealth come together and elect from among themselves the two representatives of the county. To these are at once delegated the authority and the efficacious power to authorize the freedom of their votes in Parliament.

The second are the commoners, who are those elected by the cities and other places. They are elected by those citizens who have the right to elect them under the same rules as hold for the county people in the election of the knights, only with this difference, that while these have to be natives of the county, it matters little where the others are from, provided that they are English and that the elections follow the proper procedures.

The limitation, observed in the counties and cities, of admitting to the parliamentary elections only those who have a reasonable degree of wealth, has no place in the villages, where the fewness of the inhabitants keeps out the confusion that generally arises from the multiplicity of votes. Therefore in such places everyone takes part in the election of the members.[25] Both because of the lesser expense of maintaining them and because of the advantage of having representatives familiar with the laws and understanding the affairs of the kingdom, these are for the most part persons living in London and introduced as much as possible to the business of the court.

Not all places have the right to send deputies, but only those send them which, either by privilege merited by services rendered to the crown or by ancient custom, are in this status. Because of this many communities of a few houses have a voice in Parliament,

---

[25] If Magalotti means that every man has a vote he is describing a state of affairs that did not arrive for almost two centuries.

121

and many large castles and estates have none. It is sufficient to say that this whole body is composed of about 400 people.

The lower house has no judicial functions and cannot receive any kind of oaths. Its whole task is to represent to the House of Lords the sentiments and the interests of the people. Likewise the proposals for laws that are judged useful or necessary to the kingdom are given by the House of Commons to that of the lords and by the latter to the King. If he approves them he answers in French, *Le roy le veut,* with which they at once take on the force and vigour of laws of the realm. If he disapproves, he answers in the same language that he will reflect on it, which is the same as saying "I will not have it."

The City of London

Before the fire London included 130 parish churches, of which ninety-three were burned down. According to very exact calculations the city is now thought to contain 384,000 souls.[26] Thirteen thousand houses were burned down; more than 2000 have been completely rebuilt and are lived in; five to seven thousand begun and indeed more than half-finished, over half of which will be habitable next year. Except for ceilings, joists, and flooring, wood is forbidden in the new buildings, which are all built of brick and adorned with iron balconies painted dark blue with touches of gold. The architecture is good, and everywhere there is an obligation to follow nearly the same design.

There were more than a thousand carriages for hire throughout the city before the conflagration, but now they are reduced to about five hundred, considering the lesser need for them because of the business lost from all the parts of the city destroyed by the fire.[27] They cost a shilling an hour, that is to say twelve pence, and sixpence extra for the first hour, making eighteen pence. They never charge for less than an hour, no matter how short the journey.

On the Thames there are more than a thousand boats, that is to say narrow two-oared skiffs. To cross the river costs sixpence, and the same along it from Westminster to the bridge.[28] To pass the bridge, even for only two paces, the fare is doubled. Into these

---

[26] John Graunt, *Natural and Political Observations . . . Made Upon the Bills of Mortality* (London, 1662), pp. 6–10, lists 97 parishes within the walls and 33 outside, including Westminster, Islington, Lambeth, etc. Gerald Cobb, *The Old Churches of London,* 3rd ed. (London, 1848), p. 23, says that 86 churches were burnt down or severely damaged. Graunt, *Observations,* p. 61, estimates a population of 384,000; this is for the city itself. On p. 62 he seems to say that there were one-fifth as many, or about 77,000, in the parishes outside the walls.

[27] In fact the number of Hackney coaches was strictly limited to 400 by Act of Parliament in 1662 (14 Carl. 2, cap. II); each of the commissioners who licensed coaches was to be fined £100 for each coach over the number of 400. This law also set the rates of fare given by Magalotti.

[28] London Bridge, the only one over the Thames near London at the time.

boats six people and two rowers can enter very comfortably; if there is only one rower, the charge is threepence.

At night there are boys on the corners with small link-torches to light one's way. They are paid what you please, as there is no fixed price; to be accompanied for a mile along the street you would give about fourpence. In some places there are chairs, but really not many of these; they are paid as much as the carriages, but they come out dearer, for only one can ride in them, and the carriages hold four.

The porters, who stand on almost every corner in the city, are extremely trustworthy, and are sent not only with loads but with money, letters, jewels, and every other precious thing. To go from Westminster to the city they are given a shilling, and they are obliged to bring back a written receipt from the one who has received the goods. They wear great white cloths across their chests, like a scarf, tied at the side, which they use to wrap or to hold up a load that is awkward or weighs a good deal. Before they enter the trade they have to give a good surety.

Coffee-houses are houses where coffee is sold publicly, and not only coffee but also other beverages, such as chocolate, tea, sherbets, and cock-ale,[29] cider, and others, according to the season. In these houses there are various bodies or groups of journalists where one hears what is or is believed to be new, be it true or false. In winter it does not cost more than twopence to sit at a big fire and smoke for two hours; if you drink, you pay for what you consume.

There are two playhouses and three companies of English actors. The first is called the King's company, the second the Duke's; the third is only a seminary for young actors who at times get used to the stage by reciting in their masters' theatres, and

---

[29] John Bickerdyke [i.e. Charles Henry Cook] gives a recipe for this beverage in his *Curiosities of Ale and Beer* (London, 1886), pp. 385–86: "Take a cock of half a year old, kill him and truss him well, and put into a cask twelve gallons of Ale to which add four pounds of raisins of the sun well picked, stoned, washed and dryed; sliced Dates, half a pound; nutmegs and mace two ounces; infuse the dates and spices in a quart of canary twenty-four hours, then boil the cock in a manner to a jelly, till a gallon of water is reduced to two quarts; then press all of him extremely well, and put the liquor into the cask where the Ale is, with the spices and fruit, adding a few blades of mace; then add to it a pint of new Ale yeast, and let it work well for a day, or two days, you may broach it for use or, in hot weather, the second day; and if it proves too strong, you may add more plain Ale to palliate this restorative drink, which contributes much to the invigorating of nature."

occasionally enter the two companies mentioned above. These play every day throughout the year except on Sundays, which are sanctified by everybody with superstitious devotions. On Sundays the country inns on the main roads do not give horses to travellers without special license; in London neither carriages nor chairs are for hire, so that whoever wants one has to arrange for it on Saturday evening. The taverns and the innkeepers do no business except on the sly, and keep the door shut until evening, after prayers are over for the day.

In Lent there are plays only four times a week: Monday, Tuesday, Thursday, and Saturday, and in Holy Week there are none at all.

In the theatres there is great liberty and intimacy, men and women being mixed together even in the boxes and in the large room, where one can only sit down. The women come masked to try for adventures and often succeed in forming friendships. The music of the violins is always very good. Oranges from Portugal, which here are called Chinese, are sold here throughout the year, and in summer all sorts of fruit. They play in the daytime, from three o'clock until six.

The public brothels are numerous and all very safe. These are usually the houses of the procuresses, who put you immediately into a room more or less well furnished, and bring in as many girls as you like, to show you, who go to search in the neighbourhood until one or more please you. With this they leave you alone with her and wait until they are called to send her away. But before you go they make ready on a table some ale, French wine, Rhine wine, a plate of strong oranges or at most of medium flavour, the juice of which, squeezed into ale or Rhine wine, together with fine sugar, makes a strange mixture; and for pleasure it is shared with the prostitute. There are also tarts, sweetmeats, and other trifles, so that between the pay for the girl, which regularly comes to a crown, that for the procuress, and the cost of the collation, the amusement gets away with a pound. When I said above that brothels are very safe, I meant from practical jokes, thefts, and murders, but not indeed from the French pox, for of this there is no end, and of the most treacherous and pestiferous kind.

The places called taverns are for the most part very splendid and all superbly furnished, so that persons of high rank, women as well as men, have not the least hesitation in going to them. There are also a large number of innkeepers, who in France would be called *traiteurs,* that is to say people who provide lunches and dinners. Some are English and some French, and the first gentlemen of the court go to them in the morning with the same frequency as the first gentlemen in Florence go to the inn in the evening to escape constraint and enjoy liberty. The difference between the taverns and the inns is that people usually go to the first to drink and to the second to eat. Not that one does not sometimes eat at the former and drink at the latter, but this is unusual and takes them out of their element. The truth is that both are very expensive.

There are an infinity of beer-shops where they sell many kinds of indigenous drinks, of which I have counted as many as thirty-two sorts. These places are not very expensive and so they are always full of the rabble downstairs, and upstairs of every sort and condition of persons from artisans to gentlemen. They differ from the taverns in this way, that in those are drunk Spanish wine, which is here called sack, French wine, Malaga, Bordeaux, muscat, and other costly and foreign wines, whereas in these beer-shops they drink only ale, cock-ale, buttered ale, lamb-ale.[30]

There are also common and much cheaper inns that serve for the lackeys and other poor and lower-class people. But there they eat roughly and do not drink wine. For twelve pence they will get three helpings, which all consist of beef, veal, mutton, or lamb, according to the season.

Before the fire there were six tennis courts, all of the French kind, but now there are four, the other two having been burned. The chief and finest one is that of the King, opposite the palace, with which it communicates by an overpass. The King has a changing room there, with a bed and a window from which he looks at the game from behind a grating. He usually plays there three times a week in a doublet; the guards stand at the street door, but do not refuse entry to anyone who has the face or attire of a gentleman. In St. James's park there is the King's pall-mall court, 830 measured paces long, which after that at Utrecht is absolutely the finest that I have seen.

In various parts of the city there are bowling greens. The gardens of Lambeth, of Tradescant across the river, and others near the city serve all year round as public walks for the eating-houses

---

[30] Buttered ale, "a favourite drink of the seventeenth century," was "composed of ale (brewed without hops), butter, sugar, and cinnamon" (Bickerdyke, *Curiosities,* p. 385). The lamb ale is mentioned by the same author, but with no description. It could be "lamb's wool," which was ale mixed with sugar, nutmeg, and the pulp of roasted apples.

and brothels. For the same purpose there was built a short time ago the Court of Neptune, commonly called "the Folly."[31] This is a large wooden building erected on boats, which is moved down the bank at the beginning of summer. Because the machine is so large that it is not easily moved, it is usually moored between Somerset house (which belongs to the queen-mother) and Whitehall, but on the opposite side of the river. Around it, at the level of the boats, runs a loggia with balusters, which surrounds a continuous gallery divided into more than thirty rooms, each big enough for a table and a few chairs. On the inner side each room has a door, as if to the courtyard of this palace. At the corners, on another level, there is space for four other small rooms, more retired and separate. The roofs of the structure, that is, those that go lengthwise, are arranged for playing bowls, and protected from the other two sides by wooden balustrades. Outside the whole thing is painted white, so that it resembles a luxurious casino built on an island in the river.

Three entertainments are put on in London for the lowest classes: sword-fighting, bull- and bear-baiting, and cock-fights.[32] Very large bets are wagered on each of these.

I have unfortunately never been to the first, which I imagine may be the most curious. They fight with swords having the point and edges blunted somewhat, but in spite of this they very often wound each other. The bears and bulls are led into a theatre specially built at the other side of the city, that is to say, across the river, with boxes all round. The bear is tied in the centre of this theatre on a cord long enough to let him move in a circle of perhaps seven or eight paces. Then they release some mastiff dogs, which go to attack it from the front; those who do otherwise, attacking its ears from the side, are considered no good. Now the betting proceeds. The same is done with bulls, whose horns and testicles are appropriately protected, the latter so that they may not be damaged, the former so that the dogs will not be gored when they are thrown into the air. It is indeed extremely pleasant to see them fly high up and then fall to the ground with a terrible crash, and more pleasant still to see their masters running to them; these are

---

[31] I have searched in vain for a pictorial representation of this structure. Magalotti's description is far from clear.

[32] There is much information about these spectacles in William B. Boulton, *The Amusements of Old London,* 2 vols. (London, 1901, vol. 1 reprinted 1970). It appears that the sword-fighters made private arrangements to ensure that their wounds would let a good deal of blood, but would not be serious.

butchers and similar kinds of people with whom the bottom of the theatre is full. To save their dogs from their fall they run stooping to receive them on their shoulders in the place where they are going to fall, and it often happens that the blow is so terrible that it knocks them heavily to the ground, and if several are knocked down at once near the same spot they make a very fine and ridiculous group. When the infuriated bull charges them, their flight, their shrieks, and their fear are wonderful to see.

The place for the cock-fight is a small theatre in which one sits in a circle on step-seats covered with matting. The bottom of this is a round table, of about six ells[33] in diameter and about two ells high. It too is covered with matting, all stained with the blood of the cocks. On the day of the fight, which is indicated by printed cards posted at the street corners and distributed throughout the city, when many people begin to arrive, two cocks come, carried in two sacks by two of those people who raise and keep them. One of them goes to one side and the other to the other side, and when they have taken out their birds, they hold them in their hands until the first bets are made, which everyone does according to no rules, one may say, other than their own inclination, which makes them prefer one bird to another. The cocks have their wings blunted, their crests cropped and their backs plucked; they are not of a large size, but strong and excessively courageous. Halfway down the leg they are armed with a very sharp steel spur with which, jumping into the air and thrashing about, attached to each other by their beaks, they wound each other. Parted, they watch for a little while and then crouching, return to the attack, with their necks low and stretched forward and the neck feathers standing up around their heads; thus, gradually advancing, they spring up in a flash and, driven by their wings, meet in mid-air and wound each other with their beaks, with a fury that at first gives some idea of a considerable battle. But it is true that as they tire little by little, the end becomes boring, coming down to one having to kill the other by pecking its head and eyes, which sometimes goes on for more than a good quarter of an hour and often for nearly half an hour. During the combat you hear a continuous hubbub from those who are betting, some doubling, tripling, or quadrupling their first wagers, and others laying new ones, according to how the cocks are seen to be getting on. Often when one appears vanquished and near death, it recovers such wonderful vigour that it jumps on the

---

[33] The Florentine *braccio* or ell was about 0.56 metre.

stronger one and kills it. When this happens and the defeated cock is seen to regain its courage, then the largest bets take place, one to ten, twenty, a hundred. At times it happens that both remain on the field, and while they are dying, when one falls dead the other drags himself as well as he can on to the body of his enemy and with the little breath remaining to him flaps his wings and crows his victory, after which he himself also abandons himself to death.

When one duel is finished other cocks come, as long as the people ask for them. You pay a shilling to enter, and this goes into the purse of the man who feeds the cocks for this purpose, so that seven or eight pairs of cocks, not all of which die in one day, get him about forty or fifty crowns. This race of animals is not as courageous when they are taken out of this island, as it is seen that in Normandy they do not behave the same as in England. The hatred between the cocks is natural, so that when they begin to grow larger than little chicks they are fed separately, because otherwise they would very soon kill each other.

In London there are various places where one can go for a walk with the ladies; these are St. James's park, and the gardens of Gray's Inn, Lincoln's Inn, and the Temple, which are universities where the law students stay. There are always masked women in these places, and if one wishes to begin a conversation with them he is certain not to be refused; he then succeeds in starting something else besides, and very often carries it out before evening. The carriage promenade, which begins only the Sunday after Easter and first of May, is very crowded; it takes place in the great meadow of Hyde park, going round in several concentric circles that sometimes turn out to be as many as four in number.

The Realms of Ireland and Scotland

I find that I have already said that among the greatest salaried offices that the King of England and perhaps any other Christian prince of Europe confers on a subject is the Viceroyalty of Ireland, for it should be known that the revenues of that entire realm amount to 350 or 400 thousand pounds sterling, which all pass through the hands of the Viceroy for the payment of the army and for his own emoluments, which ordinarily have no other limit than his discretion. I am told that about 1,000 soldiers, between infantry and cavalry, are paid by the King, and this is because of the necessity of restraining the country on account of the hate that the zeal of the Catholic religion instils in these people against the English and Protestant government.

The Viceroy resides in Dublin and lives with very great pomp. He has a bodyguard that gets the same pay as those of the King in London, just as all the regiments are paid the same as those in England.

In Ireland the real Irish are almost all Roman Catholics. Among the English there is the usual mixture, but the Anabaptists prevail. The tenacity of our religion comes not from zeal but from ignorance, obstinacy, and lack of will to look further. They would do the same with Hebraism if they had sucked it in with their milk. In the realm there is the same law against the Catholics as against the wolves: whoever finds a wolf gets five pounds sterling, and five pounds to him who discovers a Catholic. Even so there are more Catholics than wolves.

The people are ignorant, stolid, and weak in the head. The women have no great hesitation in having themselves covered by a brother or a cousin, but by a foreigner, watch out! There is a proverb that says, "In England the women are chaste until they are married, in Ireland when they are married, in Scotland never."

The realm has a Parliament of its own, composed of upper and lower houses, over which the Viceroy presides, and also sends acts passed by the two houses to the King for his approval and signature. However, the authority of the Irish Parliament is much

130

less than that of the English one, and in consequence the Viceroy exercises a power that is incomparably more absolute.

The army, both soldiers and officers, is mostly English, as is the greatest part of the lower house of Parliament.

Of the revenue of the realm little goes into the King's purse; indeed there is a firm belief that he makes up the necessary expenses from some portion of English money.

Scotland is not governed by a Viceroy, for the Scots claim that the King ought to reside in Edinburgh rather than in London, considering that the kingdom of England was incorporated with that of Scotland, and not that of Scotland with England. However it may be in logic, the effect is different, because when a branch of the royal house of Scotland in the person of King James came to a greater and richer country, the other came to be considered no different from a country acquired by force of arms. However, the Scots always maintain in England a commissioner or representative, who presents to the King all the business of that kingdom and although he does not hold the same post, is in effect like the ambassadors of Bologna and Ferrara to the Pope. The King keeps no minister there, if we except the particular governors of towns, who are in part Scottish and part English. Indeed he keeps an army there instead, the General of which, at present Lord Maitland,[34] a Scotsman, is in essence the Viceroy or Governor.

This man is one of the best soldiers that the King has. He has served outside the kingdom, has been Governor of Tangier, and was in the predicament of having to command that army corps that the King might have had to send to Flanders this year to help the Spanish, if peace had not been made. He usually resides at court leaving his lieutenant at Edinburgh in Scotland. The Viceroy has his bodyguards, commanded by Lord Newburgh,[35] with the same pay and perquisites as those in England and Ireland, in the same way as the mixed soldiery of the two nations, Scottish and English.

They have a Parliament composed of upper and lower houses, like those of England and Ireland, and send their acts to their commissioner in London to be signed by the King. The Scottish have the reputation of being traitors. Their character suits the policies of the French above all others, and they make a very close alliance with them. Externally their religion is Protestant, but in their hearts they are Presbyterians, and they take rather more

---

[34] John Maitand, Earl (later Duke) of Lauderdale. See note 66, p. 55.
[35] James Livingstone, Earl of Newburgh (d. 1670).

opportunities to show this than the English do in England. Some liberty is given them, thanks to the necessity of keeping that kingdom quiet, for the King cannot do at a distance what he can do in England at closer range. It may be added that the Presbyterian party is very strong, so that it becomes more expedient to look the other way. I imagine that in all Scotland scarcely three thousand Catholics could be counted.

Possessions of the English Crown Inside and Outside Europe

The three kingdoms of England, Scotland, and Ireland, set up in the realm by Clement VII in the time of Henry VIII, on whom he also conferred the title of Defender of the Faith. Henceforth he was called King of England and Lord of Ireland.

All the islands adjacent to these three kingdoms, that is to say the Orkneys to the north of Scotland, the Hebrides to the west, and other smaller islands scattered around England and Ireland; the islands of Jersey and Guernsey adjacent to Normandy, which are the relics of England's ancient ascendancy over France.

In Africa, Tangier, with some fortified place on the coast of Guinea; in Asia Bombay between Diù and Goa, given, together with Tangier, as the dowry of the present queen.

In America, Virginia, also called New England,[36] some part of Canada, and a large part of the northern continent called Greenland.[37]

The islands of Jamaica, Bermuda, Barbados, half of St. Christopher, and the other islands of the Antilles.

---

[36] Virginia was not part of New England.

[37] Of what is now Canada, England ruled only Newfoundland and a vaguely defined region around Hudson's bay. Nova Scotia had been seceded to France by the treaty of Breda in 1667. It is probable that Magalotti was confusing Greenland with the territory around Hudson's bay.

Celebrated Men of Letters in England

The list of the academicians of the new Royal Society is already being printed. This Society was set up in London under the protection of the King. Whereas this new assembly exists at present on the money that the new academicians pay to the secretary in subscribing to a sort of oath, written at the beginning of the laws of the Society and ratified by all at their entrance, they do not therefore proceed with such rigour in admitting them that they can all be considered without further inquiry to be great men of letters[38] solely because they are inscribed on that list.

It is also to be noted that as not only the desire, but also recommendation, are required for entry, there are many who do not want to decide to do it, but do not for that reason fail to be worthy men of great value. On that account I have thought it well to make a choice of those who have been accredited to me above the others by a person equally learned, dispassionate, and discreet and who knows them all by long acquaintance and experience.[39]

William, Viscount Brouncker,[40] the younger brother of Lord Brouncker,[41] who was recently condemned by Parliament as guilty of having kept the English fleet from following up the victory they had obtained in the first battle against the Dutch, having an order sent to all the flag officers in the Duke's name not to advance further. The Viscount is the President of the Society, a man of very keen judgment and of the greatest maturity. Mathematics is his strong point.

The Duke of Buckingham, very competent in chemical operations.

---

[38] All scholars were thought of as "men of letters" in Italy. This is a very acute observation of Magalotti's.

[39] The most likely informants are Henry Howard and Robert Boyle, but we have no evidence. Henry Oldenburg is another possibility.

[40] William, Viscount Brouncker, P.R.S. (1620–1684). He was the first President of the Royal Society, and a commissioner of the navy at the time of Magalotti's visit. He was the elder brother, not the younger.

[41] Henry, Baron Brouncker (d. 1688).

Robert Boyle: experimental philosophy.[42] He has written various treatises in English, some of which have been translated into Latin and some not. The titles are: *On Cold; On Colours; On the Force of the Spring Found in the Particles of Air; Attempts of Natural Experiments; The Sceptical Chemist; A Treatise Against Francis Line, Philosopher; On the Vocation of a Gentleman; On the Style of the Holy Scripture; Hydrostatics; On Substantial Forms.*[43]

One could not say so much in praise of this wise and virtuous gentleman that he would not merit much more. He is full of religion towards God, of magnanimous charity towards his neighbour, of generosity, of affability, of courtesy, of gentleness towards all. He is still quite young, but of a constitution so weak that it does not promise him all his days. He speaks French and Italian very well, but has some impediment in his speech, which is often interrupted by a sort of stammering, which seems as if he were constrained by an internal force to swallow his words again and with the words also his breath, so that he seems so near to bursting that it excites compassion in the hearer.

William, Lord Brereton,[44] very well versed in minerals and in agriculture, claims to have a thousand curious novelties concerning the multiplication of crops by soaking the seeds in some liquids, concerning the art of grafting, and the art of promoting and accelerating the maturity of fruits, and other similar observations.

---

[42] Honourable Robert Boyle, F.R.S. (1627–1691), was by far the most widely known British "natural philosopher" at the time. He was so famous that when Prince Cosimo came to England in the following year, he paid a formal visit to Boyle at his house.

[43] *New Experiments and Observations Touching Cold* (London, 1665)[Fulton 70].

Experiments and Considerations Touching Colours (London, 1664)[Fulton 57].

New Experiments Physico-Mechanicall Touching the Spring of the Air, and Its Effects (Oxford, 1660) [Fulton 13]. 2nd ed. 1662 [Fulton 14].

Some Considerations Concerning the Usefulness of Experimental Naturall Philosophy (Oxford, 1663) [Fulton 50].

The Sceptical Chymist (London, 1661) [Fulton 33].

Some Considerations Touching the Style of the H. Scriptures (London, 1661) [Fulton 41].

Hydrostatical Paradoxes (Oxford, 1666) [Fulton 72].

The Origine of Formes and Qualities (Oxford, 1666)[Fulton 77]. The treatise against Francis Line is included in the second edition of *New Experiments Physico-Mechanicall.* I cannot identify "*On the Vocation of a Gentleman.*"

[44] William, Baron Brereton in the Irish peerage (1631–1680) was a Fellow of the Royal Society, but there are no papers by him in the *Philosophical Transactions* or works in the British Library catalogue.

Isaac Barrow,[45] a good mathematician. He has printed a Euclid with a new method.

George Bate,[46] a good philosopher and physician.

Ralph Bathurst,[47] one of the King's chaplains, also a physician and philosopher of some repute.

John Collins,[48] a good mathematician, has printed several works on clocks, on navigation, and on trigonometry, all in English. He is reputed to be the greatest arithmetician in England and the man most able to give judgment on a work on geometry.

Daniel Cox,[49] a capable chemist.

George Ent,[50] a good physician and philosopher. He has published an *Apologia pro circulatione sanguinis*.

John Evelyn,[51] a great expert on agriculture and in the judgment of the English equally esteemed as a connoisseur of painting and architecture. His wife, who was brought up at Paris, paints miniatures with great delicacy.

Francis Glisson,[52] a good physician, has printed *Anatomia hepatis* and *De morbo rachitide*.

John Graunt,[53] a simple merchant who has made very curious observations on the Bills of Mortality (this is the name given in London to the reports of the parish priests, who during the recent plague were obliged to report to the office of health, or the magistrate corresponding to that, on all the dead and the diseases of which they died, each one in his parish, week by week).

---

[45] Isaac Barrow, F.R.S. (1630–1677). Elected Lucasian Professor of mathematics at Cambridge in 1663, he resigned in 1669 in favour of his brilliant pupil, Isaac Newton (1642–1727).

[46] George Bate, F.R.S. (ca. 1608–1668) was one of the King's physicians.

[47] Ralph Bathurst, F.R.S. (1620–1704). He was chaplain to the King and President of Trinity College, Oxford. He had been a physician but abandoned medicine at the restoration.

[48] John Collins, F.R.S. (1625–1683), a man of low degree who excelled in some branches of mathematics and held a number of posts, none well paid. He published several works on mathematics.

[49] Daniel Coxe, F.R.S. (ca. 1640–1730). He became a doctor of medicine of Cambridge in 1669.

[50] Sir George Ent, F.R.S. (1604–1689) was also a Fellow of the College of Physicians. The book referred to was published in 1641.

[51] John Evelyn, F.R.S. (1620–1706) is best known for his famous diary. His wife was Mary Brown, daughter of the English Resident at Paris.

[52] Francis Glisson, F.R.S. (1597–1677). His book on rickets was published in London in 1650 and his *Anatomia hepatis* in 1654.

[53] John Graunt, F.R.S. (1620–1674). He was a shopkeeper when he was elected F.R.S. in 1663. His *Natural and Political Observations on the Bills of Mortality* went through several editions, beginning in 1662.

Nathaniel Henshaw,[54] physician and philosopher, is on the point of publishing a certain method of his for changing air without changing position, from which he claims to derive very great benefit for health.

Robert Hooke,[55] a good philosopher and a good mechanician. He is the curator of the Society, that is to say it is his task to order and direct the manipulation of the experiments proposed by the academicians, after the secretary has made a choice of those that are to be made, and those that are to be rejected as useless. He has written the *Micrographia* in English.

Richard Lower,[56] one of the best anatomists in England.

Nicholas Mercator,[57] a Dane, is a mathematician and is now having a new work on logarithms printed.

Walter Needham,[58] a good physician and anatomist, has written in Latin *Disquisitio anatomica de formato foetu*.

John Pell,[59] a great theoretical mathematician, is on the point of printing an algebra with a new method.

Henry Slingsby,[60] Master of the Mint, is very knowledgeable about metals and everything that concerns the coining of money. He has a balance that is famous for its exquisite accuracy.

Thomas Willis[61] is a physician and chemist; however, he has a queer mind and is completely unsociable.

John Wallis,[62] a very great mathematician and a good philosopher.

Timothy Clark,[63] a philosopher, physician, mathematician, and a man of the highest integrity.

---

[54] Nathaniel Henshaw, F.R.S. (ca. 1623–1673). His *Aero-chalinos, or A Register for the Air,* etc., was actually published in Dublin in 1664.

[55] Robert Hooke, F.R.S. (1635–1703), one of the most versatile of men.

[56] Richard Lower, F.R.S. (ca. 1631–1691).

[57] Really Nicholas Kauffman, F.R.S. (1640–1687) best known for his map projection. The work referred to is *Logarithmotechnia* (London, 1668).

[58] Walter Needham, F.R.S. (ca. 1631–1691). The book mentioned by Magalotti came out in 1668.

[59] John Pell, F.R.S. (1611–1685) is described as proficient in seven or eight languages, besides being a mathematician and a D.D. He died in extreme poverty.

[60] Sir Henry Slingsby, F.R.S. (ca. 1621–ca. 1688).

[61] Thomas Willis, F.R.S. (1621–1675). He wrote extensively in anatomy and physiology.

[62] John Wallis, F.R.S. (1616–1703) had a good deal to do with the formation of the Royal Society. He wrote on mathematics, grammar, logic, theology, and education.

[63] Timothy Clark, F.R.S. (d. 1672), one of Charles II's physicians.

Goddard,[64] philosopher, physician, and chemist.

Thomas Henshaw,[65] a physician and knowledgeable about minerals.

Merret,[66] a physician and philosopher and a most diligent investigator of everything that concerns natural history.

Paule,[67] a theoretical and practical optician.

Francis Smethwick,[68] optician; he claims to work glasses of a regular figure different from the sphere.

Petty,[69] a philosopher and a highly esteemed naval architect.

Wilkins,[70] philosopher.

Christopher Wren,[71] mechanician, astronomer, mathematician, and philosopher.

Seth Ward,[72] Bishop of Salisbury, astronomer and philosopher.

Greatorex,[73] mechanician.

Dickinson,[74] chemist.

Browne,[75] physician and philosopher; he has written a book *On Popular Errors*.

[64] Jonathan Goddard, F.R.S. (ca. 1617–1675).

[65] Thomas Henshaw, F.R.S. (1618–1700), brother of Nathaniel Henshaw. He does not seem to have been active in science.

[66] Christopher Merret, F.R.S. (1614–1695). He apparently knew Italian, for he was one of those deputed by the Royal Society to report on the *Saggi di naturali esperienze*.

[67] Louis Paule. One of this name was elected F.R.S. in 1692, but nothing seems to be known about him. He is not mentioned in E. G. R. Taylor, *The Mathematical Practitioners of Tudor and Stuart England* (Cambridge, 1954).

[68] Francis Smethwick, F.R.S., seems to have been an amateur instrument-maker. He claimed to make lenses with non-spherical surfaces, which were several times compared with ordinary ones at meetings of the Royal Society. In 1684, we are told, he was granted a patent on his "engine" for grinding such lenses (Birch, *History*, 4, 363).

[69] Sir William Petty, F.R.S. (1623–1687), at various times Professor of anatomy and of music, political economist and naval architect.

[70] John Wilkins, F.R.S. (1614–1672), one of those instrumental in the establishment of the Royal Society. In 1668 he became Bishop of Chester.

[71] Sir Christopher Wren, F.R.S. (1632–1724). At the time of Magalotti's visit he had not yet become famous as an architect.

[72] Seth Ward, F.R.S. (1617–1689), Bishop of Exeter. Astronomer.

[73] Ralph Greatorex, (1625–1712) a leading London instrument-maker. In the manuscript as "Gretouz"; Miss Crinò's tentative identification with Adrien Auzout is untenable and unnecessary. See Taylor, *Mathematical Practitioners*, p. 229.

[74] I have not been able to identify this man.

[75] Sir Thomas Browne (1605–1682). The work referred to is his *Pseudodoxia epidemica* (London, 1646).

Streeter,[76] perspective.

Webb,[77] architect.

Wray,[78] herbalist.

Wharton,[79] physician and anatomist; he has printed a very beautiful treatise *De glandulis*.

Molines,[80] surgeon and anatomist.

Austen,[81] agriculture.

Sprat[82] writes perfectly in English. He has written *The History of the Royal Society*.

Stillingfleet,[83] theologian. He has written a book entitled *Origines sacrae*, in which there are very fine things, which have aroused more than ordinary esteem for him.

Parker[84] has written against atheists.

Owen,[85] Baxter,[86] Meriton,[87] Goodwin,[88] Benefield,[89] very learned in positive theology, and noted preachers.

Pearson,[90] a great connoisseur of Greek literature.

The Bishops of London, Salisbury, Winchester, and Armagh are very good theologians.

Sir [John] Cotton[91] has a library of manuscripts, in which there are very rare and valuable things.

Thomason[92] has a very large collection of the main notices of

---

[76] Robert Streeter (1624–1680), a painter, noted for architectural views, landscape, and still-life.

[77] John Webb (1611–1672), an established architect at the time. He had been a pupil of Inigo Jones.

[78] John Wray, F.R.S. (1627–1705). After 1670 he spelt his name "Ray."

[79] Thomas Wharton (1614–1673). The work referred to is *Adenographia: sive glandularum totius corporis descriptio* (London, 1656).

[80] James Moleyns (d. 1686) surgeon to the King.

[81] Ralph Austen (d. 1676), a writer on horticulture.

[82] Thomas Sprat, F.R.S. (1635–1713), later Bishop of Rochester.

[83] Edward Stillingfleet (1635–1699), Bishop of Worcester. The book referred to is *Origines sacrae* (London, 1661).

[84] Samuel Parker (1640–1688), Bishop of Oxford.

[85] Richard Owen (1606–1683), a Royalist divine.

[86] Richard Baxter (1615–1691), Presbyterian divine.

[87] John Meriton (1636–1704).

[88] Thomas Goodwin (1600–1680). Congregational divine.

[89] Sebastian Benefield (1559–1630) was a noted theologian, but does not seem to belong in Magalotti's list.

[90] John Pearson (1612–1686), Bishop of Chester.

[91] Sir John Cotton (1621–1709) inherited the very valuable library formed by Sir Robert Cotton (1571–1631), much of which finally went to the British Museum.

[92] George Thomason (d. 1666). His collection went to the British Museum and is known as the *Thomason Tracts*.

all the things that happened in the last twenty years, in more than a thousand volumes, large and small, of various authors.

In the house of the Duke of Norfolk[93] there are quantities of ancient statues and marbles, which are all that remains of the famous collection made by their grandfather and father, who, if I mistake not, was the Earl of Arundel.[94]

There is also the cabinet of Tradescant[95] which, if I do not err, has been published under the name of *Museum Tradescantianum*. It consists almost entirely of natural things, but to tell the truth there is nothing there that can be called rare nowadays and that is worth going across the river to see, as one has to do.

In the house of Mr. Hooke remain all the natural rarities gathered together by the Royal Society, as in a storeroom. Among these are very valuable things, and in time they will be arranged in a gallery when a building is erected in a place given them by the King two miles out of London for making their studies and holding their meetings. At present these are held in the house of the Duke of Norfolk, who has given them a site near his garden to build another structure where they can meet in winter, because in that season it would be too uncomfortable to go the one outside the city. Both these buildings await the grants promised by the King, not given them up to now.[96]

---

[93] Henry Howard (1628–1684), sixth Duke of Norfolk. See also p. 114 above.

[94] Thomas Howard (1585–1646), second Earl of Arundel. This collection is known as the "Arundel marbles."

[95] John Tradescant (d. ca. 1637).

[96] The Royal Society never got its building, in spite of the generosity of Howard. There were legal difficulties, about both the site in town and the one at Chelsea, which remained in the hands of the Society as a burden until 1682, when the King asked for its return and gave the Society £1300 for it. See Sir Henry Lyons, *The Royal Society, 1660–1940; A History of Its Administration Under Its Charters* (Cambridge, 1944).

The More Distinguished People at the University of Cambridge

Father Cudworth,[1] Professor of Hebrew.

Dr. Sheringham[2] has translated the Talmud, clarifying it with very learned annotations.

Dr. Gunning,[3] Provost of St. John's college.

Dr. Pearson,[4] Provost of Trinity college.

Dr. Sandcroft,[5] Dean of York.

Dr. Rainbow,[6] Provost of Magdalen college.

Dr. More,[7] theologian and philosopher of the greatest distinction.

Dr. Jenkes.[8]

Dr. Fleetwood,[9] in St. Catherine's hall.

Dr. Bright,[10] fellow of Emmanuel college.

Dr. Bentley.[11]

---

[1] Ralph Cudworth (1617–1688), Regius Professor of Hebrew and Master of Christ's college.

[2] Robert Sheringham (1602–1678).

[3] Peter Gunning (1614–1684), Regius Professor of Divinity and Master of St. John's college.

[4] John Pearson (1613–1686), Lady Margaret Professor of Divinity and Master of Trinity.

[5] William Sandcroft (1617–1693), Dean of St. Paul's from 1664–1668, and afterwards Archbishop of Canterbury.

[6] Edward Rainbow (1608–1684). At one time during the interregnum he had been Master of Magdalene, but from 1664 he was Bishop of Carlisle.

[7] Henry More (1614–1687), a prolific theological writer.

[8] Henry Jenkes (d. 1697).

[9] James Fleetwood (1603–1683) was Vice-Chancellor at the time.

[10] George Bright (ca. 1630–1696).

[11] I have not been able to identify this Dr. Bentley.

Professors at the University of Oxford

Theologians: Dr. Allestree,[12] Canon of Christ Church college, Regius Professor. Dr. Barlow,[13] Provost of Queen's college, Lady Margaret Professor.

For languages: Dr. Pococke,[14] Canon of Christ Church college, Professor of Hebrew and Arabic. Dr. Levin,[15] fellow of St. John's college, Professor of Greek and Latin.

Logic and metaphysics: these two professorships are not fixed, but change every year, and their election depends on the procurators of the University.

Physics: Dr. Willis.[16]

Moral philosophy: Dr. Crisp,[17] fellow of Corpus Christi college.

Law: Dr. Jenkins,[18] Principal of Jesus college.

Medicine: Dr. Hyde,[19] Principal of Magdalen hall.

Astronomy: Dr. Wren.[20]

Geometry: Dr. Wallis.[21]

History: First Professor Law,[22] musician of the cathedral of Christ's college.

University preacher: Dr. Gough,[23] a student at Christ's college.

---

[12] Richard Allestree (1619–1681), Regius Professor of Divinity.

[13] Thomas Barlow (1607–1691). He was an enemy of the Royal Society, believing that its efforts would lead to atheism or popery.

[14] Edward Pococke (1604–1691).

[15] William Levinz (1625–1698).

[16] Thomas Willis (1621–1675).

[17] Thomas Crisp (Crinò).

[18] Leolin Jenkins (1625–1685). He later became active in public affairs and was knighted.

[19] This was James Hyde (d. 1681), Regius Professor of Physic.

[20] Christopher Wren (1632–1723). At this time he was Savilian Professor of astronomy.

[21] John Wallis (1616–1703).

[22] This Professor Law has eluded me.

[23] Miss Crinò identifies this man as Stephen Goffe (1605–1681), but he had become a Catholic and was in France at this time (*DNB*)

English Poets[24]

Chaucer
Spenser
Drayton
Shakespeare[25]
Jonson
Beaumont, dramatist.
Fletcher, dramatist
Donne
Corbet
Carew
Sir [John] Suckling, a gentleman and colonel, epic poet in the style of Berni.[26]
Randolph
Cartwright
Waller, epic and lyric poet, lives in the house of the Earl of Devonshire.

D'Avenant: this man has been made a knight by the present King, lives with the reputation of being perhaps one of the greater poets of England.[27] He has the title of Poet Laureate; this is conferred by the King on one person at a time, chosen as the most worthy, and lasts for life.

---

[24] I have not attempted an extensive annotation of this section, in the belief that these names will be familiar to anyone interested, except for those whose literary pretensions have been extinguished by time. I have therefore corrected and modernized Magalotti's spellings, and confined the annotation to a very few items.

[25] P. Rebora, *Civiltà italiana e civiltà inglese* (Florence, 1936), p. 179, says that this is the first mention of Shakespeare by any Italian writer. Miss Crinò, without a reference to Rebora, makes the same statement. It is noteworthy that Milton is not in the list, but it must be remembered that he was under a cloud at the time, to a great extent because of the essay of his mentioned by Magalotti in the next section. In any event his greatest work had not yet made its effect. In his old age Magalotti began a translation of *Paradise Lost*.

[26] Francesco Berni (1497–1535). I cannot see how Suckling—or for that matter Berni—can be described as an epic poet.

[27] D'Avenant is not the only poet laureate whose reputation has faded.

Sir [Philip] Sidney, a most gentle spirit, wrote pastoral romances and some lyrical things.

Sir [John] Denham, of good family and very rich, a Knight of the Bath and Surveyor-General of Works to the king. He has translated some tragedy by Corneille.

Thomas Killigrew, was Resident at Venice, speaks Italian very well; a dramatist.

The Earl of Orrery, writer of tragedies, reputed to be one of the great talents of England.[28]

Sir Robert Howard, second son of the Earl of Berkshire; an active, but gloomy and unquiet spirit; he is in the lower house and aspires to the office of Secretary of State in place of Sir [William] Morice.

Edward Howard, his brother, dramatist.

The Duke of Newcastle has printed a famous book on the management of horses.[29] He writes plays, in which he avails himself greatly of the aid of his wife, who is said to have written two herself.

The Earl of Bristol: he also has written plays.

Dryden,[30] dramatist.

Cowley.

The memory of Mrs. Philips,[31] a poetess who died ten years ago, is famous. She was, however, very deformed of body. Among other things she translated the tragedy *Horace* by Corneille, which was represented at court this year; Madam Castlemaine, among others, acted in it.[32]

---

[28] It would be interesting to know the name of Magalotti's informant.

[29] William Cavendish, Duke of Newcastle (1592–1676). It is clear that he and his wife collaborated in his comedies.

[30] The contemporary reputation of Dryden probably depended greatly on the politics of the critic.

[31] Katherine Philips (1631–1664), the "matchless Orinda." It will be seen that she had been dead only about four years. In the words of Reverend Mynors Bright, the transcriber of Pepys' *Diary*, "the praise of her contemporaries has not been sufficient to preserve her works from oblivion" (*Diary*, ed. H. B. Wheatley, 7, 59n).

[32] John Evelyn mentions this performance in his *Diary*, February 4, 1667/8.

Index of Some Exceptional Books by English Authors[33]

A Relation of a Journey . . . Containing a Description of the Turkish Empire, of Egypt, of the Holy Land, etc. (London, 1615), was written by George Sandys.

Edward Herbert, *The Life and Reigne of King Henry the Eighth* (London, 1649).

Richard Hakluyt, *The Principall Navigations, Voiages and Discoveries of the English Nation* (London, 1589).

Samuel Purchas, *Purchas his Pilgrimage* (London, 1613).

Richard Hooker, *Of the Laws of Ecclesiastical Politic* (London, 8 parts, 1593–1597, 1648, and 1661).

The Compleat Ambassador, or Two Treatises of the Intended Marriage of Queen Elizabeth Comprised in Letters of Negotiation of Sir Francis Walshingham (London, 1665).

Robert Boyle, various works.[34]

James Ware, *De Scriptoribus Hiberniae libri duo* (Dublin, 1639).

Richard Knolles or Knowles, *The Generall Historie of the Turkes* (London, 1603).

John Gerard, *The Herball or Generall Historie of Plantes* (London, 1597).

John Parkinson, *Theatrum botanicum: The Theater of Plants, or an Herball of Large Extent* (London, 1640).

William How, *Phytologia Britannica* (London, 1650).

Sir Thomas Browne, *Pseudodoxia Epidemica: Enquiries into Vulgar Errors* (London, 1646).

Richard Norwood, *The Seaman's Practice* (London, 1637).

Sir Walter Raleigh, *Historie of the World* (London, 1614).

John Lightfoot, *Horae Hebraicae et Talmudicae* (Cambridge, 1658).

---

[33] To economize footnotes I have thought it best simply to expand Magalotti's rather cryptic references into titles cited in the usual form. I have made use of Miss Crinò's diligence in tracing some items given only by title, but in every case I have checked the result against the catalogue of the British Library or other works of reference.

[34] See note 43, p. 135.

Thomas Morley, *A Plaine and Easie Introduction to Practicall Musicke* (London, 1597).

The Countryman's Recreation, or the Art of Planting, Grafting, and Gardening in three books (London, 1640).

Sir Thomas Browne, *Hydriotaphia . . . Together with the Garden of Cyrus* (London, 1658).

Thomas Moufet, *Health's Improvement,* etc., corrected and enlarged by Christopher Bennet (London, 1655).

Thomas Shelton, *Tachygraphy* (London, 1641).

Naturae constantia by Johannes Jonstonus (Amsterdam, 1632), was later printed in English as *The History of the Constancy of Nature* (London, 1657).

England's Troubles Anatomized, by J. Cockayne (London, 1644).

Robert Hooke, *Micrographia, or Some Physiological Descriptions of Minute Bodies,* etc. (London, 1665).

John Graunt, *Natural and Political Observations on the Bills of Mortality* (first ed., London, 1662).[35]

John Roberts, *The Complete Cannoniere, or the Gunner's Guide* (London, 1639).

John Smyth, *The Seaman's Grammar* (London, 1627).

Isaac Walton, *The Compleat Angler* (London, 1653).

John Evelyn, *Sylva, or a Discourse of Forest Trees and the Propagation of Timber in His Majesty's Dominions,* (London, 1664).

Sir John Hayward, *The First Part of the Life and Raigne of King Henrie IIII* (London, 1599 [in reality ca. 1635]).

William Habington, *The Historie of Edward the Fourth King of England,* (London, 1640).

John Wilkins, *An Essay towards a Real Character and a Philosophical Language* (London, 1668).

Ephraim Pagitt, *Christianographie* (London, 1635).

S. Carrington, *The History of the Life and Death of Oliver Cromwell late Lord Protector* (London, 1659).

James Heath, *Flagellum, or the History of the Life and Death, Birth and Burial of Oliver Cromwell,* etc. (London, 1663).

Thomas May, *The History of the Parliament of England which Began November the Third MDCXL* (London, 1647).

Semper iidem, or a Parallel between the Ancient and Modern Phanatics (London, 1661).

Honorius Reggius (pseud.), *De Statu Ecclesiae Britannicae hodierno Liber Commentarius* (Dantisci, 1647).

---

[35] There were revised editions in 1662, 1665, and 1676.

Marchmont Nedham, *A Short History of the English Rebellion* (London, 1661).

Dudley Digges, *The Compleat Ambassador,* etc. (London, 1655).

Richard Ligon, *A True and Exact History of the Island of Barbados* (London, 1657).

William Molyns, *Myotomia, or the Anatomical Administration of all the Muscles of an Humane Body,* etc. (London, 1648).

Sir William Dugdale, *The Antiquities of Warwickshire Illustrated; from Records,* etc. (London, 1656).

Sir William Dugdale, *The History of St. Paul's Cathedral in London,* etc. (London, 1658).

Sir Edward Peyton, *The Divine Catastrophe of the Kingly Family of the House of Stuarts, or A Short History of the Rise, Reign, and Ruins Thereof* (London, 1652).

John Jones, *Judges Judged out of Their Own Mouth* (London, 1650).

John Weever, *Ancient Funeral Monuments within the United Monarchy of Great Britain and Ireland, and the Ilands Adjacent,* etc. (London, 1631).

John Selden, *Titles of Honour* (London, 1614).

John Selden, *Dissertatio de decimis* (London, 1617). A reply to this was written by Richard Montague, *Diatribe upon the First Part of the Late Historie of the Tithes by Selden* (London, 1621).

Sir William Sanderson, *A Compleat History of the Lives and Reigns of Mary Queen of Scotland and of her Son . . . James the Sixth* (London, 1656).

Sir William Sanderson, *A Compleat Historie of the Life and Raigne of King Charles from his Cradle to his Grave* (London, 1658).

(John Greaves), *A Discourse of the Romane Foot and Denarius* (London, 1647).

John Minsheu, *An English Dictionary* (London, 1632).[36]

John Minsheu, *A Dictionarie in Spanish and English* (London, 1599).

John Wynell, *Lues Venerea* (London, 1660).

J. Jonstoni, *Notitia regni mineralis seu subterraneorum catalogus cum praecipuis differentiis* (Leipzig, 1661).[37]

The Cabal, or the Letters of the Queen of England.[38]

---

[36] Not in the British Library catalogue nor in the U.S. Union Catalog.

[37] Johannes Jonstonus is described in the catalogue of the British Library as a Polish M.D.

[38] This may refer to *Cabala, sive Scrinia sacra, Mysteries of State and Government,* etc. (London 1654, 2nd ed. 1663).

Christopher Bennet, *Tabidorum theatrum* (London, 1656).

Thomas Gage, *The English American . . . or A New Survey of the West Indias,* etc. (London, 1648).

John Wray, *Catalogus plantarum circa Cantabrigiam nascentium* (Cambridge, 1660–1663).

Francis Glisson, *Anatomia hepatis* (London, 1654).

Francis Glisson, *De rachitide* (London, 1650; 2nd ed. London, 1660).

Walter Needham, *Disquisitio anatomica de formato foetu* (London, 1667).

Thomas Willis, *Pathologiae cerebri* (Oxford, 1667).

An Introduction to Algebra Translated out of the High Dutch by T. Braucker, . . Augmented by John Pell (London, 1668).

Thomas Wharton, *Adenographia* (London, 1656).

James Usher, *Britannicarum Ecclesiarum antiquitates* (Dublin, 1639).

Clement Walker, *The History of Independency* (London, 1648).

John Greaves, *Elementa linguae persicae* (London, 1649).

John Wallis, *Grammatica linguae anglicanae* (Oxford, 1653).

Henry Spelman, *De non temerandis ecclesiis* (London, 1613; Oxford, 1646).

Robert Burton, *The Anatomy of Melancholy* (Oxford, 1621; London, 1652, 1660).

Thomas Sydenham, *Methodus curandi febres* (Amsterdam, 1666).

Sir Edwin Sandys, *Europae speculum, or a View and Survey of the State of Religion in the Westerne Parts of the World* (The Hague, 1629).

John Selden, *The Privileges of the Baronage of England When They Sit in Parliament* (London, 1642).

John Milton, *The Tenure of Kings and Magistrates: Proving That it is Lawfull . . . To Call to Account a Tyrant, or Wicked King, and After Due Conviction to Depose and Put Him to Death* (London, 1649).

Thomas May, *Historiae parliamenti Angliae* (London, 1650).

George Bate, *Elenchus motuum nuperorum in Anglia. Pars prima. Pars secunda* (London, 1663).

John Coke, *Sylloge variorum tractatuum* (London, 1663).[39]

Clement Walker, *The Compleate Historie of Independency* (London, 1660).

---

[39] I have not been able to identify this.

Samuel Hartlib, *The Husbandry and Natural History of Ireland* (London, 1659).[40]

Christopher Merret, *Pinax rerum naturalium Britannicarum* (London, 1666).

George Sandys, *A Relation of a Journey begun An. Dom. 1610,* etc. (London, 1615). [Many other editions].

The Earl of Sandwich has many very valuable manuscripts concerning navigation.

---

[40] This may refer to Gerard Boate, *Ireland's Natural History . . . Now Published by Samuel Hartlib* (London, 1652).

The More Famous Artists of London

Painters

Lely:[41] his profession is portraiture, at which he is excellent. He has never been in Italy, but in spite of this his manner can be said to be very good, as it has spirit, strength, and splendour. The King is having him do a very beautiful picture, showing a sort of Arcadia in which all the most lovely ladies of the court and of London will be shown as nymphs, and life-size. I have seen the sketch, which is very fine.[42] Lady Castlemaine did not want to be in it, saying that she would be mixed up with so many women, without one man. This painter is very rich and lives like a noble. He owns very fine pictures by the best Italian masters. He is perhaps forty-five years old but handsome and courteous to the highest degree. He does marvellous pastels. A head costs twenty pounds.

Cooper:[43] he does miniature portraits wonderfully well. He gets paid thirty pounds each for them and pretends to do you a great favour. A little man full of spirit and courtesy. He also is very rich and in his house lives no less honourably than Lely. He works on a table covered with velvet, edged with gold lace, and keeps his shells of colour in the most delicate little ivory boxes. His brushes are in grenadilla wood. In short, greater delicacy could never be seen.

---

[41] Peter Lely (1617–1680), knighted by Charles II in 1679. Of Dutch origin, he moved to England in 1640, and enjoyed the patronage of Cromwell as well as of both Kings.

[42] Mr. Oliver Millar, an authority on the paintings in the royal collections, tells me that he knows of no other reference to this projected *Arcadia* or of any painting that could be associated with it.

[43] Samuel Cooper (1609–1672), called by one authority the greatest painter of miniatures who ever lived. The price of thirty pounds was paid by Samuel Pepys on August 10, 1668 for a portrait of his wife. But the Grand Duke of Tuscany, Cosimo III, who had sat for his portrait during his visit to England in 1669, paid £150. See Anna Maria Crinò, *Fatte e figure del seicento anglo-toscano* (Florence, 1957), pp. 324–35.

Helst:[44] he is esteemed for his miniatures, but I have seen neither him nor any of his works.

Pierre Damian,[45] a Frenchman. He works very well making portraits in enamel; they cost from seven to twelve pounds a piece, according to size.

Viola Players

Cristofano Semproni, a very old man; he is a Catholic, and a printer by trade.

Banister;[46] I do not know him.

Sir John Belles.[47] This is a gentleman who was at Florence at the time of the wedding[48] and had the honour of playing in the chamber of the most serene Grand Duke.

John Smith; he also has been in Italy.[49]

George Wash.

Stewkin of Hamburg.[50]

Francesco Corbetti of Padua, for the guitar.[51]

Telescope-makers

Richard Reeves:[52] to the reputation of this man that of his father, who died two years ago, has greatly contributed. The latter

---

[44] Miss Crinò's identification of this painter with Bartolomeus van der Helst cannot be right, for he was living in Holland at this period. A possible candidate is John Hayls (ca. 1600–1679), who painted Samuel Pepys' portrait in 1666, but neither Hayls nor van der Helst was a miniaturist.

[45] I cannot identify this artist.

[46] John Banister (1630–1679), violinist and composer; at this period leader of the King's band.

[47] Sir John Bolles, Bart., an amateur violist to whom Christopher Simpson dedicated his famous book *The Division Viol*, 2nd ed. (London, 1665). Sir John had recently been in Italy.

[48] Presumably the wedding of Prince Cosimo of Tuscany and Margaret of Orleans, which took place in 1661.

[49] One John Smith, violist, was in the King's band in 1667–1668, indeed from 1660 until 1673, when he "was forced to retire on account of his religion" (H. C. de Lafontaine, *The King's Musick* [London, n.d.], p. 384).

[50] Probably Theodor Steffkin, one of a family of musicians in the service of the Stuart kings (De Lafontaine, passim).

[51] One "Frasico Corbett" played the guitar at a performance of a masque in 1674 (De Lafontaine, p. 281).

[52] Richard Reeves, who probably died in 1679, was, in fact, one of the leading optical instrument-makers of his century (see E. G. R. Taylor, *The Mathematical Practitioners of Tudor and Stuart England* [Cambridge, 1954], pp. 223–24). The reference to his father is obscure, but his son, John, followed him in the business. Prince Cosimo bought a burning-glass from him, but he had to dun Cosimo (then Grand Duke) to get paid for it. (*BNCF,* MS Gal. 286, 53r.)

made those two famous microscopes with which were observed the things that were seen in print all over Europe. One of these microscopes is in the hands of Boyle, the other in those of another gentleman whose name I forget. However, he does very good work, although a long way from marvellous in my estimation. I really do not know the price of his telescopes. He sells microscopes for four pounds; those of a new invention, which folds everything into the support.[53] He is indeed a very courteous man, obliging and easy to deal with.

Clockmakers

Samuel Betts.[54]

Jeremiah Gregory.[55]

Mr. Hooke has found a way of giving pocket watches the benefits of the pendulum.[56] He, nevertheless, calls them pendulum watches, but I would call them watches with a bridle, because the time is regulated by a little tempered spring wire, with one end attached to the balance, the other to the barrel of the watch. Now this works in such a way that the to-and-fro motions of the balance are always equal, and if some irregularity of the cogwheel should cause it to gain, the spring holds it under control, obliging it to go always at the same speed. They say that if it is hung up or on a table the invention works well and really corrects the defects and irregularities of the wheels, not less well than the pendulum, but if it is carried in the pocket the temper of the

---

[53] This feature has generally been dated much later.

[54] Samuel Betts, an early member of the Clockmakers' Company, had his shop at the back of the Exchange.

[55] Jeremiah or Jeremie Gregory (d. 1685), master clockmaker in 1665; his shop was in the Royal Exchange.

[56] Magalotti described this in a letter to Cardinal Leopoldo de' Medici on February 21,/March 2, 1667/1668, which is in Florence, Bibl. Naz., MS Gal. 278, 151r–152v, and was published by A. Fabroni, *Lettere inedite d'uomini illustri*, 2 vols. (Florence, 1773, 1775), vol. 1, pp. 298–301. It was nearly all translated by R. D. Waller in *Italian Studies*, 1 (1937), 53–55. It has been pointed out that there is nothing about this in the minutes of the Royal Society for that date, and that Magalotti's account substantiates Hooke's later accusation that the Secretary, Henry Oldenburg, did not enter the minutes correctly (Sir Henry Lyons, *The Royal Society, 1660–1840, A History of Its Administration Under Its Charters* [London, 1944], p. 88). This passage is also of interest because, with the exception of the first two lines, in which Hooke is identified, it corresponds almost word for word with the letter to Leopoldo. This is one more confirmation that Magalotti was the author of the *Relazione*.

spring alters according to the heat that it feels and lets the balance run more freely.

Engravers on Copper
Faithorne.[57]

For Mathematical Instruments
Sutton.[58]

Thompson.[59]

Finally I am glad to add John Kendal the famous master bootmaker. He lives in the street of the King of France's flag. Three pounds sterling a pair.

At Oxford there is a very good draughtsman in Flemish crayon who does portraits; he gets two and a half pounds. There is another who has the secret of colouring marble in such as a way that the colour applied externally penetrates a good deal inwards, but not too much.

---

[57] William Faithorne the elder (1616–1691).

[58] This should be Henry Sutton, who was renowned for the accuracy of his scales; but according to Taylor, *Mathematical Practicioners,* p. 220 he had died in 1665.

[59] Probably Isaac Thompson, who was an assistant to Sir Samuel Morland at the time of Magalotti's visit (Taylor, *Mathematical Practitioners*, p. 266).

Beautiful Ladies of London

In conclusion I know no better way of closing these recollections and repairing the taste of those who have had the patience to read them just as they have come from my pen with the shortness of time that always distresses a traveller, than to oblige myself to pronounce the names of the fairest and most charming ladies of London.[60]

I protest that from first to last I have written them down in the order in which they came to mind. I ask pardon of those who are omitted, assuring them that they have not been left out because of envy or spiteful thoughts, but only because of my misfortune that has not perhaps let me know and admire them all in such a short time.

Frances Theresa Stuart, Duchess of Richmond and Lennox.

Miss Stuart, her sister.

Lady Castlemaine.

Miss Wells, maid-of-honour of the Queen. [They say that this one has had a son by the King.][61]

Miss Howard, maid-of-honour of the Duchess.

Miss Churchill.

Mrs. Middleton.

Mrs. Robartes.

Mrs. Russell.

Miss P. Wilmer.[62]

Mrs. Carey.

Miss Floyd.

Lady Shrewsbury: her husband challenged the Duke of Buckingham five months ago because of her and was wounded and then died.

---

[60] This whimsical piece of effrontery on the part of Magalotti need not detain us. Many of these ladies can be identified in the *Memoirs of the Comte de Gramont*.

[61] The sentence in square brackets is from Miss Crinò's decoding of a passage in cipher.

[62] "Perhaps Lady Whitmore, one of the "beauties" painted by Sir Peter Lely." (Crinò).

Miss Howell and her cousin.

Lady Carnegie.

The Viscountess of Halifax.

Miss Regnal.

Miss Gray.

Miss Diana Verney, daughter of the Earl of Bedford.

Mrs. Hungerford;

Mrs. Henrietta Hyde, wife of the second son of the Earl of Clarendon, the former Chancellor.

The two Fanshawe sisters.

Two other sisters, the Moynings.

Lady Payne.

Lady Southwell: doubtful, the court being divided between those who think her very lovely and those who consider her reasonably ugly. She is the wife of Sir Robert Southwell, who was in Florence for a long time and now is being sent to Portugal for the second time by his King.

INDEX OF PERSONS

The list of poets, pp. 143-44, the authors of the books listed by Magalotti, pp. 145-49, and the "beautiful ladies of London," pp. 154-55, have not been indexed. Names occurring in footnotes have been indexed only exceptionally.